CUBAL ANALYSIS
A Post Sexist Model of the Psyche

Karin Blair has developed a tool for men and women to use in understanding themselves that breaks through limited male-oriented concepts of Freud and Jung. As a model, the cube is a marvelously functioning three-dimensional coordinate system arrayed in relation to the axes of age, sex, morality. At different points in their lives people will find themselves in relative closeness to youth versus age, masculinity versus femininity, and goodness versus badness. By using the dynamic structure of the cube, individuals can gain access to all the polar dimensions of the cube, which creates a vivid experience of integration within.

With crystal-sharp intensity and clarity Karin Blair sets forth the theoretical background for her concepts and games that can be used in working with the cube. She also demonstrates how she has used cubal analysis in personal crises as well as with groups, particularly one adapting to the dislocations of a foreign culture.

CUBAL ANALYSIS

A POST SEXIST MODEL OF THE PSYCHE

BY KARIN BLAIR

MagiCircle
PRESS

 For information address Magic Circle Press, 10 Hyde Ridge Road, Weston, Connecticut 06883.

Cover design: Ken Daly

Composition: Fairfield County Typographers

Library of Congress Catalog: #82-62051

For Jay and Ann

Acknowledgments

The people who have helped me with this enterprise are many. A complete list would have to begin with those who have already mentioned in my book *Meaning in Star Trek,* where the cube first took shape. However, those having a special relationship to *Cubal Analysis* include: Teacher and psychologist, P. J. Manion, of the Union Graduate School and the Jung Institute in Zurich; psychologist, Christian Mathyer of Geneva; administrator and communications expert, John Rider of Webster College, Geneva; women's studies scholar, Jean Martensen of Geneva; psychologist, Friedemann Wieland of Munich; editor and humanities expert, Roy Fairfield of Union Graduate School, Cincinnati; psychologist and teacher, Hannah Levin of the Union Graduate School, Cincinnati; black studies expert, Vincent Harding of Union Graduate School, Cincinnati; psychologist, Jonathan Klate from Massachusetts; teachers Teresina and Joseph Havens of Temenos, a retreat center in western Massachusetts where one can have the experience of "just being;" writers Pat Boughton and Ralph Hummel of Urbia Associates, New York, and finally neighbors Mary Richards and Angela Cook who have used their intuitions and typing skills in laying out and typing the final version.

There are also several institutions which deserve special mention: Union Graduate School; The University of Geneva; The Jung Institute of Zurich where I have studied; College Rousseau, College de Stael and Webster College in Geneva where I have taught; The International simulation and Gaming Association; The European Association for American Studies and The Etudes Pedagoguiques of Geneva where I have made presentations. Wilson College and Indiana University have helped me obtain articles and other bibliographical materal that otherwise would have been very difficult to find.

Last but not least I want to thank my family who as always have helped in so many ways, large and small. I am reluctant to single out those daily domestic activities which we have all shared so that each has the time and space for other activities. Making a point of them when performed by someone other than the mother/wife implies that basically the woman is the one responsible for their execution. Nonetheless I am grateful for having had the "room of my own" within which to work. My daughter, Ann, helped me a great deal with the typing of semi-final drafts from earlier drafts only a daughter could read or a mother love. Her energy for finishing up whatever was started often took mine in tow when it was running low. Her sense of irony also helped me keep even the most rushed and hectic moments in some kind of perspective. My husband, Jay, was always willing to listen to my gropings and read my drafts. Ready with incisive criticism he encouraged me to sharpen my focus and my prose.

Although burdened with an unusually busy period professionally, he too found the energy to support me when it seemed as if I would collapse before I finished.

Having thanked the major people and institutions which have contributed to this project, I also want to mention the many synchronicities, the strokes of luck and happy coincidences, which have lightened and enlightened hard human labor.

CONTENTS

Preface

Central to "Cubal Analysis" is the notion of the cube. Its three-dimensional mathematical symmetry provides a backdrop against which to gain perspective on recent psychological models of mental space. Beginning with the theories of Otto Weininger who crystallizes the ideas prevalent at the turn of the century, I then move into the theories of Freud. In relation to women Freud through the technique of the case history at least permitted to women as well as men a linear development through time. His former student, Jung, however, began to address himself to more fundamental issues moving away from unbalanced conceptions of women. His psychic models took "evil" as a reality and not merely as the *privatio boni*; similarly in his quadratic view of the psyche women had their own place and the feminine was more than simply the absence of the masculine. To Jung's essentially two dimensional conceptions, Perls adds emphasis on dynamic change. A continuum of awareness replaces static conceptions.

The theory I put forth to extend this progression into the present is based on the three-dimensional balance of the cube. As human beings, we must live in a three-dimensional world and cope with the three inescapable axes of our existence: morality, age and sex. Using these three dimensions as the structuring principle of the cube, the eight apexes acquire the following definitions: the good old woman, the good old man, the good young woman, the good young man, the evil old woman, the evil old man, the evil young woman, the evil young man. These apexes represent parameters of our psyche as it takes shape in the world around us. As a mathematically symmetrical model the cube invites us to counteract the skew of personal and cultural interpretation. Although traditional morality has attempted to keep many of these character types either hidden or out of relationship with those which are more highly valued, the demands of growth and process if not progress oblige us to relate all these possibilities to each other. Whereas evil has traditionally been seen as a *privatio boni*, the feminine as lack of the masculine and age as a waning of youth, the cube invites our full attention to both poles of each axis. We are encouraged to move beyond the limitations of either-or thinking to conceive of gradations on continua, the poles of which can emerge into a full manifestation of their qualities. The *I Ching* as a *Book of Changes* provides a model for relating all of the various combinations to one another. It places our Western character type in a matrix for change and interrelationship; in addition our imaginations can perhaps make more relevant a network of archetypes initially clothed in obscure oriental imagery.

In the first part of the manuscript I trace the theory and evolve the cube; in the second part I apply it to two specific contexts. First, I use it as a conceptual tool for dealing with the crisis of women who move from culture to another. Second, I use it as a device to understand and eventually resolve the major crises of my personal life which occurred at moments of entry or reentry into a new culture. In the third part I present practical ways I have used this model as a basis for games. In the first part then the intellectual framework is elaborated, in the second it intersects with the social and the personal dimensions cast into relief by culture change, in the third it intersects with the unknown as it emerges in the process of gaming and of interacting with others.

In this last part of the twentieth century there is a need for a context independent of social prejudices within which to understand oneself in all of one's diversity. We can no longer believe in the "naturalness" of inherited cultural patterns nor in the "goodness" of those who would assert absolute "truths." The cube is my attempt to answer the challenge this situation poses.

> *The meaning of my existence is that...I myself am a question which is addressed to the world, and I must communicate my answer, for otherwise I am dependent on the world's answer.*
>
> *C. G. Jung.*

Introduction

We in this century have an unprecedented self-awareness and consciousness of our psychological processes. Whereas the psyche was formerly in the domain of religion, Sigmund Freud opened it up to investigation and created theories which still have an impact on many whether or not they are pursuing therapy. Nonetheless his concepts are marked by the moral climate of his time, so clearly expressed by Otto Weininger, his contemporary. Whatever their personal or social origins they continue to have an impact which is not only personal but social as well.

As a woman I am especially concerned with the evolution of influential twentieth-century models for the human psyche and their impact on conceptions of the feminine. In the course of the following manuscript I set up a mathematical model, the cube, which by being three-dimensional and symmetrical provides a conceptual frame of reference in terms of which the gaps in influential concepts of the psyche become obvious. Starting from the theories of moralist Weininger I move through those of Freud to explore the important additions made by his former student C. G. Jung. It is at this point that I move from Jung's more balanced notions to my own concept of the fully three-dimensional cube. This then is enriched by the works of Fritz Perls who added to static concepts of the psychological tradition the importance of change and process, which moves us into the fourth dimension. In this perspective I refer to the Chinese classic, the *I Ching* or *Book of Changes*, to recapitulate the movement we have followed through increasingly complex notions of the psyche and to provide a model which has room for archetypes in a context of constant change.

The recognition of the importance of change rather than the staticness of conceptions is a recent phenomenon for our culture and women have been the most touched by the imbalance which static ideas and ideals have imposed. In so far as Motherhood defined their role and significance, women had to live in a one-dimensional world. This is where we start with Weininger. From there Freud by permitting personal history to man and woman alike moved into two dimensions, adding that of time to sexual reproduction. Jung finally addressed openly the problem of symmetry by means of his theories of archetypes as symmetrical formative elements. In doing so he insisted on the presence of the feminine as significant in and of itself, more than simply the absence of the masculine. However, he was limited by his concept of "wholeness" which maintained a sense of a goal, a concept or ideal toward which one progresses, often defined in terms of the male, "the higher Adam," for example. Perls takes a major step forward when he sees everything in terms of foreground and background, in terms of a dynamic interrelationship of needs and their fulfillment. Since goals and needs necessarily change as we do, an adequate concept of the psyche must incorporate the expectation of change and some means of open-ended exploration of it analogous to the role of chance in the *I Ching*. In the context of Perls all sexual differences are treated on the purely personal level where they are more appropriate, i.e., in terms of who was attracted to whom sexually.

As a culmination to this tracing of twentieth-century psychic models as they relate to women and concepts of the feminine, the cube functions as a three-dimensional and symmetrical metaphor which can accommodate change and give to women as well as the feminine, the evil, and the old a psychic space equal to that of men and the masculine, the good and the young. With its help in Part II I analyze "crises" as conflicts between polar opposites on the cube. Crucial moments of conflict have become most dramatic and evident at moments of moving from one culture to another one, both in my own life and in those of other women who left their home cultures to come to Geneva. The cube has served me well as a tool for analysis and for synthesis; with its help I have had a model for examining the external world and evaluating the options it presents; and with its help I have been able to create an inner space capable of fruitfully seeing opposites as gradations on continua rather than destructive oppositions.

Part I

In reality, a good three weeks were still to pass before I could truly make up my mind to live again. I could not eat because all food repelled me. The view of city and mountains from my sick-bed seemed to me like a painted curtain with black holes in it, or a tattered sheet of newspaper full of photographs that meant nothing. Disappointed, I thought, "Now I must return to the 'box system' again." For it seemed to me as if behind the horizon of the cosmos a three-dimensional world had been artificially built up, in which each person sat by himself in a little box. And now I should have to convince myself all over again that this was important! Life and the whole world struck me as a prison, and it bothered me beyond measure that I should be finding all that quite in order.

C. G. Jung

1
Cubal Geometry

Jung in his sixties had a near fatal heart attack during which time he experienced himself in another realm. As he describes this state:

> There was no longer anything I wanted or desired. I existed in an objective form; I was what I had been and lived.... There was no longer any regret that something had dropped away or had been taken away. On the contrary: I had everything that I was, and that was everything.[1]

From the confines of his hospital room, that "box" less binding only than that of the coffin, Jung experiences another dimension of existence which has the quality of eternity. Thirty years earlier he had had a similar experience when he returned to the garden of his childhood and to a special stone "'which stood in some secret relationship to me....'"[2] He reexperienced this earlier relationship in which he and the stone talked to each other and the boundaries separating them became obscure. From this perspective his life in Zurich seemed remote and alien to him. "This was frightening, for the world in which I had just become absorbed was *eternal*.... I had to tear myself violently from the spot in order not to lose hold of my future."[3]

From those two experiences of another dimension to life we can see Jung's ambivalence toward the "box system." On being called back to this state after his heart attack, Jung perceived three-dimensionality itself as a kind of stage prop through which people isolate themselves in little prison-like boxes. On the other hand, he was aware of this condition as necessary to his hold on his future. Even at sixty, his recovery was followed by considerable creative activity. He still needed his three-dimensionality as a stage on which to act and as a metaphor for his models of the psyche. A comparable ambivalence emerges on other manifestations of box or cube conceptions, particularly the cubiculum.

The word "cube" as contained in cubiculum has a comparable ambivalence. Cubiculum is first of all a burial chamber, the ultimate in enclosed and confining prison-like spaces. However, it also means sleeping chamber, the place of dreams, and chapel, the place of prayer. Thus the cube can be not only a prison but that special "place of predilection"[4] where one can tap those special inner spaces such as Jung rediscovered in the garden of his childhod. Such spaces are intersections between worlds, between the three-dimensional "box system" and another temporal dimension which touches the unknown.

The word "cube" derives from the Greek, "kubos," meaning die. A die was thrown or cast to determine an outcome. A three-dimensional object by being set into motion intersected with time and the unknown. As a gambling device it evokes the purely fortuitous, but since the arbitrary is an element in symbol formation,[5] it also touches the oracular and symbolic. The cube as die is then a three-dimensional device for reaching beyond its own dimensional limitations.

To the dot the line is liberation, to the line the plane is liberation, to the plane the cube is liberation, to the stationary cube the moving cube is liberation. Each step by incorporating the unknown generates a new dimension. As we saw in the ambivalence of Jung's attitude to the "box system," man needs both a tool for structuring his universe and then a further development of that tool for moving beyond the limitations of his own creations. The cube as box is an easy image for the needed structuring device, the room we all need to survive; the cube as die permits an intersection with the unknown, a moving beyond established limits.

The need for going beyond the dimensional limits inherent in any particular conceptual scheme is evident in the following mathematical reflection:

> A race of two-dimensional men might live in every one of a pile of a million sheets of paper, and it would be physically impossible that they should ever communicate or even be aware of the possibility of each other's existence, though the distance separating any two would be less than the thousandth of an inch. So, three-dimensional universes may be packed closely together in four-dimensional space, and we may be surrounded—almost touched—by myriads of beings like ourselves, of whose existence we are unconscious and into whose sphere we cannot come.[6]

Our minds are in perpetual danger of being trapped in the dimensions of our own conceptions—if we take them to be final. The cube as a three-dimensional framework has particular reinforcement in the modern world—cubic rooms are stacked into cubic buildings which in turn form city blocks. Such is the common image of the grid which dominates modern industrialized cities with its network of uniformly spaced horizontal and perpendicular lines. It has been criticized because "all vestiges of the mythopoeic, synchronistic, spiritual whole...are denied in the rational, linear and secular world view of the grid."[7] However, there is not necessarily such a dichotomy between spiritual "wholeness" and everyday "partialness." We create that opposition just as we create our everyday world. Since the shapes we surround ourselves with reflect and are reflected by our mental structures, we tend to live mentally and physically in cubes. We are physically three-dimensional beings who live in cubic spaces and judge the world around us in terms of the boxes we made physically and mentally. If we accept these constructions of ours as establishing the ultimate limits of our lives we are as stuck as the pile of two-dimensional men living on sheets of paper dreaming perhaps of a three-dimensional spiritual whole. Such is the situation portrayed in the following song.

Little Boxes[8]

In the city, on the hillside,
Little boxes made of ticky tacky,
Little boxes, little boxes,
Little boxes all the same.
There's a green one and a pink one,
And a blue one and a yellow one,
And they're all made of ticky tacky,
And they're all just the same.

And the people in the houses
All go to the university,
And they all get put in boxes,
Little boxes all the same.
And there're doctors and there're lawyers,
And there're business executives,
And they're all made out of ticky tacky,
And they all look just the same.

And they all play on the golf course,
And drink their martinis dry,
And they all have pretty children,
And the children all go to school,
And the children go to summer camp,
And then to the university,
And they all get put in boxes,
And they all come out the same.

And the boys go into business,
And marry ands raise a family,
And they get put in boxes,
Little boxes just the same.
There's a green one and a yellow one,
And they're all made out of ticky tacky,
And they're all just the same.

In the song "Little Boxes" the box or three-dimensional cubic form of the room becomes a metaphor for the subdivision house which resembles every other, which in turn becomes a metaphor for the minds of the people inhabiting the houses who by never questioning conventional categories and values also look just the same. The same shape, that of the cube or room or house could however become sacred space by focusing on the liminal or threshold space in which one can move between worlds rather than on the enclosed contained space. Similarly traditional or conventional mental categories can be used as tools for exploring the unknown, for going beyond the boundaries such categories can create *and* extend. Einstein lived in a house that was probably more or less square and went to school. He used his physical and temporal spaces as creative tools in a changing world rather than as confining definitions in a static one.

Edward Albee in his play, "Box," dramatizes how even extreme boxed-in-ness can surpass its own limitation. A box is the only character; it speaks, significantly, with a woman's voice. The world represented is one in which art has been reduced to craft as exemplified in the construction of the box. There is room enough for a rocking chair in the box, and room enough to move around in, "take a turn," but no room for the unknown, "the dice so big you can hardly throw them any more."[9] Beauty, that release of tension by returning to order, "no matter how far traveled...on its own terms"[10] can only remind one of the unattainable.Nonetheless something stirs inside the box as she has visions of the sea and fog and birds; "Look; more of them; a black net...skimming. And just one...moving beneath...in the opposite way."[11] She wonders how it can be; "the memory of what we have not known becomes the needed complement to the fully closed system represented by the box and are implied by it.

Similarly, as we shall see, the cubal conceptions proposed in this study also depend on necessary limits which it becomes necessary to transcend in time. But first of all it is important to acknowledge the positive function of conceptional models as expressions or vehicles for human cultures. All culture is based on codes of communication which in turn are based on paired relationships between the message and the interpretation, the thing and its meaning.[13] The same thing, the same message or sign can exist in many different contexts or cultures but its significance will differ according to the rules by which it is interpreted. For example, the letter "a" exists in many words in many languages; its meaning depends on the rules which govern its position and function in a word. Without these basic structures which cultures perpetuate there can be no communication between people; however, without the opportunity to play with their limits new dimensions of oneself remain inaccessible. Jung's encounter with death made him aware of other dimensions more acutely than he had been. Few people, however, want to confront themselves for fear of facing their own mortality. One of the primary functions of the "box" is to restrict one's awareness of what might otherwise be threatening; similarly one major function of cultural conceptions is to screen out reminders of one's mortality. As long as one can believe that one's cultural conceptions define reality, one can enjoy a security based on the consensus shared with one's compatriots. One has access to an eternal and unchanging cultural reality which whatever its limitations is easier to accept than one's individual human death.

One of the functions of culture is to create the basic structures within which its members must live, psychically and physically. Architectural styles differ from culture to culture as do value systems and cosmologies, all of which are artifacts. In *Denial of Death* Ernest Becker treats in detail the problem of the "cultural lie," that set of rules whose function is to set up the fictional framework within which members of a given culture can distinguish themselves from members of other cultures and from nature. The lie is as arbitrary and artificial as any set of rules and through its function of giving meaning takes precedence over the natural reality of fellow humans and the physical environment.

> The fact is that this is what society is and always has been: a symbolic action system, a structure of statuses and roles, customs and rules for behavior, designed to serve as a vehicle for earthly heroism.Each script is somewhat unique, each culture has a different hero system. What the anthropologists call "cultural relativity is thus really the relativity of hero-systems the world over...in which people serve in order to earn a feeling of primary value, of cosmic specialness, of ultimate usefulness to creation, of unshakable meaning. they earn this feeling by carving out a place in nature, by building an edifice that reflects human value.... The hope and belief is that the things that man creates in society are of lasting worth and meaning, that they outlive and outshine death and decay, that man and his products count.[14]

The function of culture is to elaborate the terms through which a person may attain significance. Taking the individual human as comparable to any of a number of natural "facts" the function of culture is to establish the rules which by governing his/her behavior provide the framework defining "good" and "bad". These rules function like the grammar rules by which any given letter can have significance. The first threat to such a meaningful life is the spectre of death and decay, against which most cultures seek to protect themselves through claims to eternal values. thus culture is first of all at odds with nature whose mysteries force one to confront the facts of life and death. Within a given culture people are linked to one another by loyalty to certain notions of heroism even as they, like sibling rivals, compete for recognition and achievement in terms of that heroism. Distance from nature marks high status: dignitaries are transported by others and dressed so that the slightest dirt would be evident if it were present whereas the low status of the laborer is dramatized by his proximity to dirt, the earth, the body. Polarization is built into the functioning of the cultural lie, the social fiction by which the good is separated from the bad.

Since polarization is essential to cultural lies, the cube offers a way of organizing conceptionally the essential polarities of human life. Like the sphere, the cube offers the possibility of directional orientation without making any one direction or orientation predominant. Whereas the pyramid has a top easily assimilable to whatever is seen as culturally "good," the cube as die has only that "top" arrived at through any given throw or intersection with the unknown. Any given apex can be arranged to function as the top of a pyramid would; however the individual must take the responsibility for any given arrangement and in fact create the secondary structure which will mainain the cube on end.

The utility of dealing with a three-dimensional conceptual structure is pleasantly dramatized in the hypothetical problem with which Martin Gardner begins *The Ambidextrous Universe*.[15] Man is attempting to communicate with intelligent life elsewhere in the universe and first of all must indicate how the message is to be read. Since reading necessitates distinguishing back from front, up from down and left from right, the problem of dealing in three dimensions is immediately invoked. We must assume gravity elsewhere in the universe to establish a sense of up and down; we must assume locomotion elsewhere in the universe to provide the sense of front and back; however there is nothing in the physical universe to which we can turn to establish the difference between left and right. The distinction is inescapably cultural.

If one wishes to generalize from this starting point the three dimensions of living become the spatial, the temporal, and the cultural, through which one distinguishes between left and right, bad and good. The *I Ching*[16] to which we will turn in greater detail in Chapter 7 elaborates this cosmology in terms of plants, animals and finally humans. Plants then live only in one dimension and through gravity relate to "up" and "down." Animals in addition to verticality have horizontal locomotion which permits them to relate to "front" and "back"; in human terms this involves a sense of time, often measured in terms of motion, and providing a sense of "future" and "past." In addition to these two dimensions humans by means of the "cultural lie" distinguished between "good" and "bad," "right" and "left." Plants grow through time; animals add locomotion; as humans do moral considerations. In human terms then I would like to see sexual differences, which are based on spatial configurations as characteristic of one dimension. Aging would be a function of time and moral differentiation that of culture. In terms of a cube each of these becomes one of the three constituitive axes. Temporal differentiation yields age and the opposite poles of young and old; spatial differentiation yields sexuality and the opposite poles of male and female; culture differentiation yields mortality and the opposite poles of good and bad.

Each of eight apexes refers to a possible conjunction of the polarities involved. There is the apex of the good old man , that of the good old woman, that of the bad old man, that of the bad old woman. Studying the distinctions and the relations between these three axes and eight apexes allows us to investigate fruitfully cultural phenomena both psychically and socially.

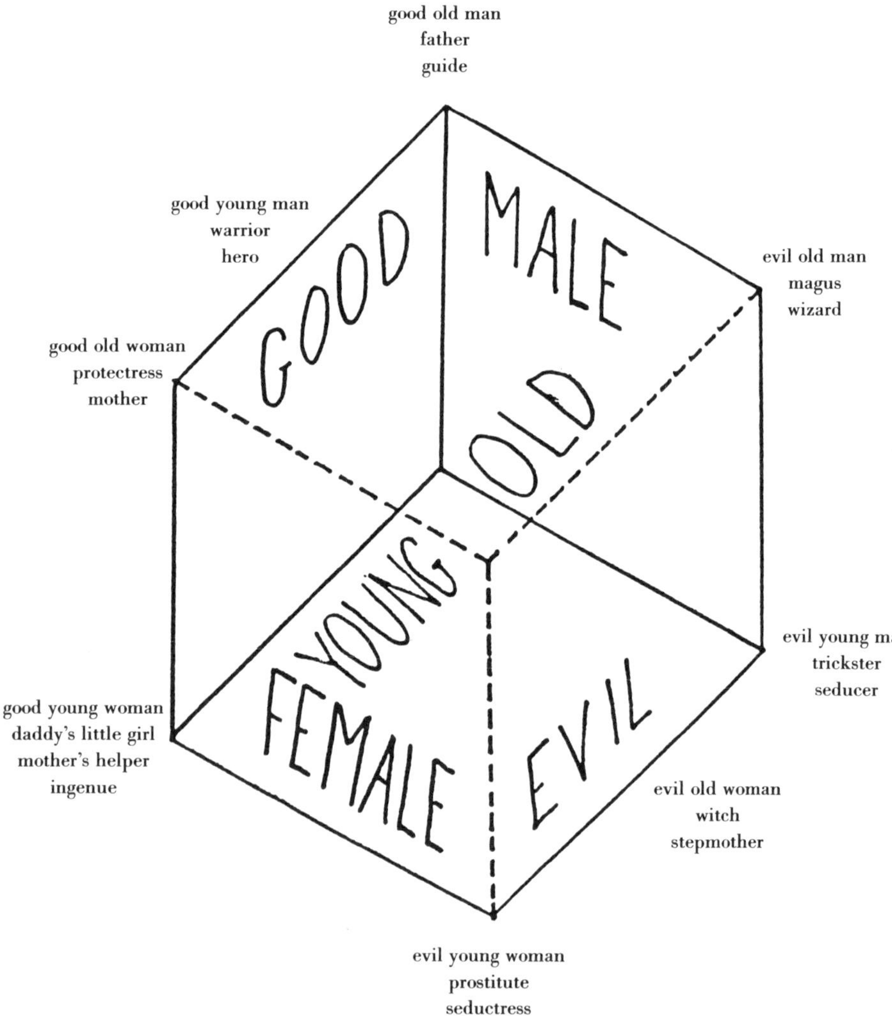

Being a mathematical model this conceptual cube produces a complete and symmetrical universe in relation to which the asymmetries of the actual world become more obvious. Although symmetry may not be the principal which guarantees motion and change,[17] nonetheless mathematically symmetrical models serve as indicators of as yet undiscovered or unincorporated material.

> The advantages to research are gained from the way that a regular pattern reveals gaps where, if the pattern is consistant, something new ought to be found. The teaching advantages spring from the way a suitable framework makes things fit together so that connections between ideas are easy to memorize.[18]

In terms of our world today where woman's issues are catalyzing changes occurring now in relation to concepts of "nature" and "culture," key problems for everyone, one of the functions of the cube can be to reveal asymmetries between the sexes which are of particular interest to me as a woman. for example, if value were distributed equally among the apexes of the "good" face of the cube, male and female would have equal access to it; however, such is clearly not the case. To return to the terms elaborated by Becker, evil is ultimately that which reminds us of our mortality, therefore women traditionally do not share equally in the availability of cultural value:

> The real threat of the mother comes to be connected with her *sheer physicalness.* Her genitals are used as a convenient focus for the child's obsession with the problem of physicalness.... He sees her tie to the earth, her secret bodily processes that bind her to nature: the breast with its mysterious sticky milk, the menstrual odors and blood, the almost continual immersion of the productive mother in her corporeality, and not least—something the child is very sensitive to—the often neurotic and helpless character of this immersion...the mother must exude determinism, and the child expresses his horror at this complete dependency on what is physically vulnerable.[19]

Female sexuality as a locus of that mysterious life-death force becomes the antithesis of culture, of the fictions by which we try to free ourselves from body determinism. The very fact of two sexes confronts one with the arbitrariness of the body; the child "understands that the particularity of each sex is a limitation of potential, a cheating of living fullness in some ways."[20]

Biological arbitrariness is enhanced by the overlay of cultural lies which interpret the body's "significance." One body, that of the female, is made to bear the burden of all animal nature while that of the male comes to represent the outside world of symbolic significance which triumphs over nature. This evaluation of woman is according to contemporary structuralists essential to culture. Culture, as we saw, was based on rules for determining the value and function of any given entity. Exchange systems derive immediately from such rules which establish who pays whom, how much and for what. However

> ...according to Levi-Strauss..., the ultimate basic symbolic exchange which provides the model for all the others is sexual. The incest taboo...implies a capacity to distinguish between women who are permitted and women who are forbidden and thus generates a distinction between women of the category *wife* and women of the category *sister.* The basis of human exchange, and hence the basis of symbolic thought and the beginning of culture, lies in the uniquely human phenomenon that a man is able to establish a relationship with another man by means of the exchange of women.[21]

Sexual differentiation has rarely considered precise genital description: on a philosophical level it has been based on the idea of the complementarity of the sexes; on a social level it has been based on the utility of one sex to the other. Masculine activity has to be completed by female passivity in order to have a field for its enterprises. Philosophical complementarity is necessary to social utility. The activity of the sperm is given cultural significance, that of the egg which descends the fallopian tubes none; the activity of the penis during orgasm is given significance, that of the vagina which contracts none. The penis, a tube that hangs out, is no longer simply another body part like the liver or spleen or vagina, a tube that hangs in; rather it becomes a magic wand, a bearer of symbolic significance with which to transform the natural world. Rationally the world could just as well be divided on the basis of those whose belly buttons stick in and those whose stick out.

The very elaboration then of the discovery between masculine and feminine functions as one of a series of cultural lies or fictions meant to distance one from the threat of body awareness, body determinism, mere nature. It is therefore absurd to look to such distinctions for information on the physical difference between the sexes. Masculinity and femininity are categories meant to remove us from the biological facts and from the fact of biology. Nonetheless the entire moral and conceptual code which underlies Western psychological models is colored by this dichotomy. The gender difference is all the more pervasive when the psychological theory places great emphasis on sexuality, as does that of Freud.

As a woman I am especially concerned with the evolution of influential twentieth-century models for the human psyche and their impact on conceptions of the feminine. Here again the cube is a most useful conceptual device. By using the mathematically symmetrical universe of the cube as a conceptional frame of reference, gaps in recent psychological theories become evident. Starting from the theories of the moral philosopher Otto Weininger, I want to show in the next sections how important psychological models of this century move toward and into three-dimensional concepts and finally incorporate change itself into the model.

Notes to Chapter 1

1. C.G. Jung, *Memories, Dreams, Reflections*, ed. Aniela Jaffé, trans. Richard and Clara Winston (Glasgow: Fountain Books, 1977), p. 322.
2. Jung, *Memories*, pp.20-1.
3. Jung, *Memories*, pp. 20-1
4. Carlos Castenada, *Journey to Ixtlan*, Touchstone,1972, pp. 184-189, as cited in Mimi Lobell, "Spatial Archetypes," *Quadrant*, 10, No. 2 (Winter 1977), 17.
5. Edmund Leach, *Culture and Communication*. (Cambridge: Cambridge Univ. Press, 1976,) p.12.
6. H. Bruce Franklin, *Future Perfect*, rev. ed. (New York: Oxford University Press, 1978), p. 363.
7. Lobell, *Quadrant*, p. 36.
8. "Little Boxes" sung by Pete Seeger on *Strangers and Cousins*, CBS Stereo SEPG 62528. Song written by Malvina Reynolds.
9. Edward Albee, "Box," in *Tiny Alice, Box, Quotations from ChairmanMao Tse-Tung* (Harmondsworth: Penguin Books, 1971), p. 128.
10. Albee, p. 130.
11. Albee, p. 132.
12. Albee, p. 131.
13. Dan Sperber, *Rethinking Symbolism*, (Cambridge: Cambridge Univ. Press, 1975,) p. 14.
14. Ernest Becker, *The Denial of Death* (New York: the Free Press, 1973), p. 5.
15. Martin Gardner, *The Ambidextrous Universe* (New York: Basic Books, 1964), p. 1.
16. *I Ching*, (Princeton: Princeton Univ. Press, 1967,) p.263.
17. Fritjof Capra, *Tao of Physics*, (Boulder Colorado: Shambala Press, 1975,) p. 257.
18. J.L. Jolley, *The Fabric of Knowledge*, (London: Duckworth, 1973), foreword.
19. Becker, p. 39.
20. Becker, p. 41.
21. Edmund Leach, *Claude Levi-Strauss*, (Middlesex England: Penguin Books, 1976,) p. 45.

2

The Dot: Weininger

At the turn of the century Otto Weininger in *Sex and Character* elaborated a moral code which was to influence both Freud and Jung, the main architects of twentieth-century psychology. He laid out the characteristics of masculine and feminine in terms overlapping with what would later be called the conscious and the unconscious; the extremeness of the gap which separated them is a result of an imbalanced moral perspective depending on the notion of evil as merely the absence of good. The violence of the gap might be seen in his premature death by suicide at the age of 23 and as posing the essential terms of the challenge to which subsequent thinkers had to address themselves. Evil as *privatio boni*[1] guarantees that the opposites good and evil are mutually exclusive, a position characteristically Western. In the East the yin and the yang, while opposites, each contain elements of the counterpart, whereas in the West opposition is assumed to be exclusive. Weininger elaborates this assumption more starkly than most in his life as well as his work. He states for example that

> blood transfusions should be carried out only within each sex: since all cells of the female body were female, their being set free in the individual male system, as in all social systems, would cause an immediate internecion.[2]

Such is the completeness with which he sees masculinity as excluding femininity and both as being differently embodied in actual men and women.

Otto Weininger was born in Vienna in 1880 and shot himself twenty-three years later shortly after the publication of his book, *Sex and Character*, in which he collapses the basic distinction between masculinity as the sole reality and femininity as non-masculinity. At times he gives his theory the misnomer of bisexuality which Freud used, attributing it at times to himself, at times to Fliess.[3] By bisexuality Weininger wished to establish that women when they exhibit any positive characteristics such as intellect have a masculine side. However, since femininity is the absence of masculinity, men need not be bothered by what has no essential existence.

In these terms the man is the "monad," the "basic unity," (O.E.D.) or that "elementary unextended spiritual substance from which material properties are derived." (Webster) Man then is like the primordial circle which perhaps because of its perfect symmetry has in nearly all times and places symbolized unity and totality, "heavenliness." Man then as the basic unit of reality creates not only his own reality but also that of woman who is nothing in herself but the expression and projection of his sexuality. Woman then is like the dot at the center of the circle, nothing itself. It is the circle not the dot that makes the center. She in order to maintain her existence must continually kindle his sexuality through her desire for him as phallus, as magic wand calling her into being. She is totally dependent on man and incapable of making use of any creative energy except as a means to the end of pairing. "Woman is the sin of man."[4] She is his ineradicable lower part, the matter which "appears to be as inextricable a riddle as form, woman as unending as man, negation as eternal as existence, but this eternity is...that of guilt."[5]

Since woman's essential nature is negation, matter and guilt, the highest praise that can be given her is to say that she is like a man although no woman can in his opinion ever aspire to masculine creative power. To try to do so would simply plunge her more deeply into womanliness.[6] She cannot change.

Within this world where the good is masculine consciousness and the bad is its negation embodied in the feminine, Weininger makes one further set of distinctions. Among men there are two basic types: the genius and the politician; among women the two types are the mother and the prostitute.

The genius and the mother are concerned with the furtherance of the race. The mother produces children to this end, making her personal body the means of her contribution to the course of human life. The genius through his consciousness and his will affirms the entire universe in the individual. He has a perfect memory independent of time and a consciousness that see all at a flash.[7] Since evil is *privatio boni*, the notion of the immoral genius, the great evil one, is only a myth made to scare timid folk.[8] The genius because of his consciousness cannot be bad, the mother because of her unconsciousness cannot be good.

The prostitute and the politician differ from the mother and the genius in their concern for personal power and freedom rather than the concerns of the race. While the mother and genius work for the future in silence, the prostitute and politician are indifferent to the objects of life. If the child is the goal of the sexual act for the mother, sex is for the prostitute its own reward. If the mother treats her lovers as sons, the prostitute treats her sons as lovers. If the mother is the safe harbor from which men set sail, the prostitute is the woman met on the high seas, the siren who stimulates self-consciousness. If the mother is given to men materially, the prostitute relates to them intellectually and is necessary to the mental completeness of the genius.[9] The politician like the prostitute needs a public to function; however, since he is conscious, he like the genius is basically good. The role of the genius is to spiral around all the possibilities that life has to offer and to relate to both the mother and the prostitute since sexual ripeness defines them both and neither can change or grow.

The genuis is the circle, the true self-contained microcosm, the sublime orchestration of differentiation and distinction, individuality and discriminaton. Though the politician is more limited, both masculine types are linked to consciousness and the good: hence there is no polarization between them. They differ from each other in terms of their goals; the politician acts in the world for rewards to himself, the genius acts for rewards to posterity without thought for himself. The woman, however, whether as mother or prostitute, is the unconscious, hence immoral, undifferentiated dot who is perpetually lost in a state of indistinct fusion with others. Both as prostitute and as mother she is defined in terms of her relationship to men; the prostitute is a necessary mirror for the man's refinements and caprices, the mother is a source of necessary materials for man's projects and goals. The woman is the vanishing point on the horizon in relation to which the dominating masculine eye can establish its sense of perspective. Between the two, the vantage point and the vanishing point, everything in the world can be arranged in a static and precise relation to everything else.

Although traditionally we are accustomed to extreme moral polarization between the mother and the prostitute, we can see in Weininger's work a conceptual merging of the two which is resurfacing now through the women's movement. Since both are dependent adjuncts to men for whose service they are in some way purchased, some women are saying today that in terms of possibilities for self-definition and independence both are in fact prostitutes, both are for sale. In Weininger's terms since neither has access to consciousness or to will and hence to the categorical imperative, neither is capable of moral action. Since both are defined in terms of their bodies, both are equally unconscious and both are purchased for essentially the same reason: the prostitute for the physical pleasure of her sexuality, the mother for the fertility of her sexuality.

Although Weininger talks about masculinity and femininity as being components of everything in the world, he also locates them respectively in men and women. The male monad as essential spiritual substance which creates the world, becomes one with the conscious world. The woman as complement is nothing and therefore evil as absence of good, as if Weininger wished to make evil vanish through the vanishing point. A more viable perspective, as we shall see, emerges in Jung. For example, Jung, when asked whether or not he thought there would be a third world war, responded that he thought that would depend on there being enough people who could stand the tension between opposites. In his opinion survival itself depended on embodying a complementarity rather than on exclusivity between opposites.[10]

A tendency to radical division between opposites has contributed to exaggerated imbalances in the West. In the East the "monad" or basic unity was both nothing and everything. Whatever was brought to consciousness differentiated itself from the potentionality from which all life flows. Symbols of this unity such as the mandala or magic circle were seen as conscious constructions and used as meditation devices through which the mind might be revealed to itself. All such concepts and constructs were seen to reflect the working of the mind and were not asked to corrrespond to nature or reality. An important goal in their use was to free the individual from the network of words or concepts which consciousness had spun, from *maya* or illusion, so that one might experience the flow of life in that moment. Such constructs were never asked to correspond to an empirical reality available to the senses. The individual never assumed s/he could know *the* perspective along which to arrange the world.

Although Weininger makes the distinctions essential to the three axes of the cube, his world remain monistic because of the way in which the axes function. Masculine/male and feminine/female correspond to consciousness/good and unconsciousness/bad. Thus we have seen women can never attain to consciousness and goodness just as men can never fall into unconsciousness and evil. Since women are defined by their sexually mature bodies, youth and age are irrelevant to them; in addition they cannot change. Thus time is irrelevant to women though not to men who are permitted a spiral evolution within the sphere of consciousness. In this way all three axes remain for women in one bundle, which viewed from the male vantage point appears as a mere dot.

As we will see in the next section Freud continues many of Weininger's conceptions; nonetheless his techniques and their assumptions open the door to a new dimension available to women as well as men. Freud continues to identify the masculine as the positive and conscious with the feminine as its complementary negative and unconscious defined in terms of missing masculinity, but he also sees personal history and the concomitant possibility of evolution through time as esential to both men and women. In this way his psychological model incorporates an important new dimension.

Notes to Chapter 2

1. Thomas Aquinas, "Summa Theologica," *Introduction to Contemporary Civilization in the West*, vol. I, (New York: Columbia Univ. Press, 1960.) pp.208-214.
2. Mary Ellman, *Thinking About Women.* (New York: Harcourt Brace Jovanovich, 1968.) p. 69.
3. Sigmund Freud, *Trois essais sur la sexualite* (Paris: Gallimard, 1932.) and Ernest Jones, *The Life and Works of Sigmund Freud.* (New York: Basic Books, 1961.) p. 205.
4. Otto Weininger, *Sex and Character* (London: William Heinemann, 1906.) p. 299.
5. Weininger, p. 300.
6. Weininger, p. 341.
7. Weininger, p. 182.
8. Weininger, p. 182.
9. Weininger, p. 276.
10. Barbara Hannah, *Jung: His Life and Work.* (New York: McGraw and Hill, 1977.) p. 129.

3
The Line: Freud

If with Weininger the male consciousness was identified with the basic spiritual unity, relegating the unconscious and the feminine to non-existence, Freud enlarged reality to include the unconscious. Although he would have liked to have seen evil as that which was not yet assimilated to consciousness, he had to admit its reality too in his later years. Thus Weininger's monadic world moves into two dimensions. With Freud the ego can trace a line of development between the conscious and the unconscious.

Although Freud admits the unconscious into the real world, it remains a function of consciousness in so far as it is made up of material that the ego rejects and represses. Thus he shares with Weininger an unquestioned positive evaluation of consciousness. The conscious ego can pursue the cultural ideal, the superego, which determines what is repressed and what not. In so far as the unconscious is made up of the rejected fragments of consciousness, it is to the conscious mind as looking-glass image is to the figure in front of the mirror. Were the figure not there, the mirror would be empty.

Whereas Weininger did not see the need for contact with an unconscious to which he in fact attributed no reality, Freud developed a technique intended to reestablish a contact between the conscious and unconscious which had been broken off. The individual through psychonalysis can choose to reclaim material that had been repressed into unconsciousness. Thus the sharp metaphysical break in Weininger's world between good and evil, masculine and feminine, conscious and unconscious can be bridged by a line of personal history which psychoanalysis can help to unfold. Weininger's suicide might be seen as a sign of such an absolute and unacknowledged break in his world. Whereas for Weininger the negative was feminine matter, for Freud the unconscious was described in terms of the body which determined woman's nature but was shared by both sexes. The id is that sum of needs, drives, urges, instincts which derive from biology and provide the driving force for one's life. If for Weininger the line between culture and consciousness is absent, for Freud the superego as cultural ideal is distinct from the individual human ego which can then choose to repress or reclaim the unconscious. Both Freud and Weininger, however, see the will as the key to conscious identity. According to Freud, the individual represses that which s/he does not wish to be, probably because it would conflict with the ideal of the world structured by a masculine God who called it into being by an act of will and proceeds to shape it by means of intellectual distinctions. In both it is the human will which links man to the moral ideal, which to Weininger alone confers humanity. Although Freud gives substance to the unconscious, he does not give it positive value but considers it a kind of slagheap of repressed and discarded material. Whereas Weininger's genius is consciously concerned with the course of the human race as the mother is unconsciously, Freud wants to see all polymorphous sexual pleasure focused into the genitals so that all sexual energy is first of all directed to reproduction and then through sublimation into cultural pursuits. Everyone is by now familiar with his claim that the girl at puberty must cease to be concerned with her clitoral pleasure and transfer the center of activity to the vagina so that she can become the mother which will then define her role. There is a similar claim that men too must undergo a comparable intensification of focus so that orgasim becomes *the* goal of all sexuality. Although the man is left his sexual pleasure and energy which he can sublimate or not, the woman is left with only the cultural role which values fertility at the cost of sexuality. Both sexes, however, are asked to focus their sexual energy as a function of will in the service of a cultural ideal.

Freud in giving the unconscious more substance than Weininger similarly grants more of an existence to women. Nonetheless he continues to define them in terms of their lack of masculinity, whence penis envy. Although he elaborates on Weininger's theory of "bisexuality," he remains within the hold of past bias in affirming the reality of masculinity which some women may exhibit elements of. Similarly, by limiting female sexuality to fertility, Freud cuts women off from cultural libido which he in fact says is characteristic of males. As with Weininger women can reproduce human raw material but they cannot produce the cultural ideals which can give meaning. Similar implications can be found in the emphasis on the Oedipus complex and in the absence of a comparable "myth" for women as we shall see shortly.

As originator of the psychoanalytic movement Freud saw himself as rejecting existing cultural explanations of man in order to analyze regions of the human being thought to be the sacred preserve to religion. Giving reality to the unconscious and opening avenues to it permitted radical changes in Weininger's conception of the psychological universe. Whereas the unconscious had been seen as evil, that is, defined by absence of the good or the cultural ideal, now it was a new territory available to the individual human ego. Freud states that the intention of psychoanalysis is

> to strengthen the ego, to make it more independent of the superego, to widen its field of perception and enlarge its organization so that it can appropriate fresh portions of the id. Where id was, there ego shall be.[1]

This statement has revolutionary implications from the point of view of a traditional society in which the superego or cultural ideal defined the shape and function of the ego. For example, in Weininger the categorical imperative awakening man's will to the ideals of humanity is the vehicle of consciousness. On a less lofty level, social institutions establish themselves in some continuous way and focus on recognized purposes in terms of which participants have defined roles. By decreasing the dependence of the ego on the cultural ideal or superego, one automatically diminishes the force of the shared expectations which bind individuals to the institution in question. Once the ego has perceived itself as possible script writer, it has also perceived alternatives to the scenarios handed on by traditions.

Having created alternatives to traditional scenarios himself, Freud proceeded so far beyond tradition as to see himself as the unfathered founder of psychoanalysis: "Freud had soared so far beyond his natural family that it is no surprise that he should indulge in fantasies of self-creation."[2] But, of course, to the extent that he could see himself as self-created, Freud would escape the rebellious logic of the Oedipal situation.

Eric Neumann points out that traditions in which the firstborn son was sacrificed might well express paternal ambivalence toward the son who could one day threaten to replace the personal father and the cultural past he represents. The Oedipal drama reverses this situation and through Freud's canonization of it supports the emerging consciousness of the son, symbolized by his killing of the father. The importance of the symbolism of the situation can be seen in the relations between Freud and Jung. Although "fatherless" Freud nonetheless needed sons and sought them through the movement he began. Creator of his own world, he nonetheless sought heirs for his creation.

> Freud was looking for an heir, and it was Jung who was to be the 'son' whom he

> had proudly chosen as his spiritual successor and who would assure the success and continuation of psychoanalysis.[3]

Seeing himself as fatherless, Freud had no one behind him and was doubly vulnerable to rejection by the son, a rejection which would call into question the significance of his work. Thus when Jung began publishing articles expounding psychoanalysis without mentioning Freud, the master felt profoundly threatened. His first reproach to Jung for doing this preceded his falling over in dead faint, after which he accused Jung of harboring "death wishes" toward him. Jung defended himself by saying "Why should I want him to die? I had come to learn. He was not standing in my way; he was in Vienna, I was in Zurich."[4] As Becker points out, Jung acknowledges his role as learner but at the same time expresses his intention to stand on his own in a relationship of equality to Freud. By standing on his own Jung would be threatening rivalry with Freud and denying him an "heir."

Freud in fact canonized the Oedipus relationship and in doing so was canonizing his relationship to the "father" of past traditions, that "whole mysterious and dark past of mankind that psychoanalysis was chosen to decipher."[5]Although his schema of the psyche has space for women, they are still defined by dependence and lack. The Electra complex which attempts to fulfill a comparable function for women was rejected by Freud since it would make female experience distinct from male experience.[6]

In spite of Freud's rejection of the "Electra complex," attempts have been made to use the story of Electra as a model for the experience of women. Even so it fails to provide a comparable model for female self-definition and therefore leaves the resulting image of woman within the already existing manmade categories. Whereas Oedipus kills the father and takes over his "territory" including the mother, Electra helps Orestes, her brother, kill Clytemnestra, their mother, and Aegisthus, her lover, to avenge the murder of their father. First of all Electra does not kill Clyemnestra herself and second she does not gain access to the father or to the mother's lover or any of her "territory." Electra does not claim possession of a cultural identity which came to her through the mother, nor does she undertake her own *causa sui*, her own self-definition in distinction to that of her mother. In any case this cultural lie is a creation of the male mind and thus part of the patrimony. What could a mother leave beyond matrimony and motherhood?

The desire to create oneself and the negative attitude this entails toward the woman as mother is eloquently expressed in the following quotation by Antonin Artaud.

> ...it is not just Jesus Christ whom I want to seek out among the Taranumaras but myself, me, M. Antonin Artaud born 4 September 1896 at Marseilles, 4 rue de Jardin des Plantes, from an uterus that I had nothing to do with and with which I have never had anything to do before, because to be copulated and masturbated for nine months by the membrane, the brilliant membrane which without teeth, devours, as the UPANISHADS say, is no way to be born and I know that I was born in another way, through my works and not from my mother, but my MOTHER wanted to take me, and you can see the result in my life. I was born from my sadness alone and would that you could do the same too, M. Henri Parisot. And we must believe that the uterus approved this sadness, since it wanted to take it for itself and feed off it under the guise of maternity.[7]

Mother is the ultimate threat to self-definition which men see as their main life work. What, however, happens to a woman's desire for self-definition if in terms of our man-made cultural canons all women are defined by their sexuality and potential if not real motherhood? Where are the cultural tools which encourage woman to achieve independence from mother and most of all from the ideas surrounding motherhood?

Although Freud and Weininger, like Artaud, are concerned with their own *causa sui*, their self-propagation, and make woman dependent on man in their theories, Freud's techniques permit him to transcend his ideas. Whereas Freud in theory kept woman dependent on his notions of sexuality and myths for consciousness, in practice he initiated techniques equally available to either sex. Freud's most equitable contribution lies in the realization that an individual's development must be understood in terms of that person's history. He coined the hybrid word—case history[8]—and in doing so asserted that all general cases have their reality in terms of some specific history. Through the process of therapeutic self-examination, of analysis of the past, of free association on one's memories, one can hope to create a future which is different from the past. On the one hand this technique of psychoanalysis offers to men and women alike the possibility of self-recreation; on the other hand uninterpreted facts are meaningless and we must recall Einstein's saying that it is the theory which decides what we can observe. Thus although Freud gives women access to the specifics of their experience, he limits the possible significance of that experience by the theories he expounds for its interpretation. It is as if he gave to woman a movie camera with which to recreate herself and her life but at the same time created a scenario which made sense from only one vantage point, that of the man.

Thus, despite advances in our conception of women, traditional conceptions of consciousness/unconsciousness, masculine/feminine, good/evil continue to dominate in spite of Freud's techniques and of his embodying a commitment to self-definition. Although Freud in his later years came to be more pessimistic about the possibility of evil or unconsciousness being safely kept within the individual sphere, his original theories remain influential. The unconscious remains a mirror image of the ideal projected by the conscious mind. Just as a lack of a penis is essential to the "configuration of femininity,"[9] so lack of good is the essential element in evil, and lack of consciousness is the essence of unconsciousness. Although the case history and the possibility of personal change through psychoanalysis are available to men and women alike, Freud himself can say of his future mother-in-law:

> I do not think I am being unfair to her; I see her as a person of great mental and moral power standing in our midst, capable of high accomplishments, without a trace of the absurd weaknesses of old women, but there is no denying that she is taking a line against all, like an old man. Because her charm and vitality have lasted so long, she still demands in return her full share of life— not the share of old age—and expects to be the center, the ruler, an end in herself. Every *man* who has grown old honorably wants the same, only in a woman one is not used to it. As a mother she ought to be content to know that her three children are fairly happy, and she ought to sacrifice her wishes to their needs.[10]

Unlike Oedipus, the individual conscious male, who distinguishes himself from the father, no individual woman, even one of "great mental and moral power," distinguishes herself from the mother. In spite of the fact that Freud's theories liberate the axis of temporal evolution for both sexes, his opinions remain within the mental set of Weininger: a woman's motherhood still defines her even in old age when fertility is no longer relevant.

Just as Freud's theories—if not all his opinions—do move beyond those of Weininger, so Jung's move beyond those of his mentor. Freud's later suspicions that all of the contents of the id or unconscious were not available to transformation by the ego and hence were not simply the results of repression were developed by Jung. Whereas Freud's confidence in consciousness expressed itself as pessimism when confronted by an inexplicable unconscious, Jung's scepticism about the scope of consciousness expresses itself in the theories which make the unconscious a source of significance. Jung expanded the notion of the unconscious and in doing so restored to it some of the mystery of which Freud had hoped to divest it. If part of Freud's burden was the degree to which psychoanalysis was a great iconoclastic movement, Jung in launching out on his own lessened his burden by making room for a meaning that can be spiritual. Jung in expanding the unconscious saw in it elements that cannot be brought to consciousness, i.e. areas of ultimate unconsciousness, followed by areas of relative unconsciousness which can be partially conscious, followed by the personal unconscious or that area which is a function of an individual's personal repressions.

Jung's enlarged image of the psyche has several important results for women. First of all he moved beyond the constraints of his culture of origin by drawing on the material of myth from all over the world. He moved outside the assumptions of a given society and even of Western culture to a notion of a humanly shared layer of consciousness. By attributing to the unconscious an independent reality, the seat of the transcendent as well as the would-be transcended parts of the past, Jung also breaks through the Western prejudice that good is only the absence of evil and the feminine the lack of masculinity. Although the majority of his actual diagrams for the psyche were two dimensional, his later reflections and some diagrams move into three dimensions. The possibility of doing so was implicit in the symmetry of his earlier concepts which gave to the masculine and feminine at least formal equality. Whereas Freud rejected the notion of a principal of feminine consciousness, an analog to the Oedipus complex, Jung's psychic models are sexually symmetrical. If the *anima* mediates consciousness for the male, the *animus* is a comparable principal of consciousness for the female. Thus while continuing to validate the temporal axis called forth by Freud's concept of the case history, Jung differentiates the other two axes by beginning to free the masculine/feminine axis from that of the conscious/unconscious. Whereas Freud's psychic progression was linear, that of the ego reclaiming the id for the greater glory of the superego or ego ideal, Jung moves in the direction of adding another dimension.

Notes to Chapter 3

1. James Hillman, "The Great Mother, Her Son, Her Hero, and The Puer," in *Fathers and Mothers* (Zurich: Spring publications, 1973), p. 104.
2. Becker, p. 110.
3. Becker, p. 110.
4. Becker, p. 111.
5. Becker, p. 112.
6. *Collected Papers of Sigmund Freud* (London: Hogarth Press, 1961), vol. V, p. 256 as cited in Barbara Engler, "Freud's Sexual Politics: Hersey of Heroism?" *Anima*, 2, No. 2 (Spring Equinox 1976), p. 68.
7. Antonin Artaud, "Lettre a Henri Parisot (7 Sept. 1875)," in *Oeuvres Completes.* (Paris: Gallimard), tome IX 64-65 as cited in Monique Plaza, "Phallomorphic Power and the Psychology of 'Woman'," *Ideology and Consciousness*, No. 4 (Autumn 1978), p. 11.
8. Engler, *Anima, p. 65.*

9. Sigmund Freud, "New Introductory Lectures on Psycho-Analysis," in *Complete Psychological Works*, vol. XXII, p. 132 as cited in Mary Ellmann, *Thinking About Women* (New York: Harcourt Brace Jovanovich, 1968), p. 154.
10. *The Letters of Sigmund Freud*, p. 38 as cited in Ellmann, p. 132.

4
The Square: Jung

Freud added an essential dimension by separating out the axis of time through giving significance to personal history; Jung begins to differentiate the sexual and moral axes despite considerable ambivalence on his part. This ambivalence shows up when we study Jung pursuing a mathematically perfect form such as a cube. As a model it has the advantages of revealing the gaps where something new might well be found. Another advantage is that it reveals ambivalences and inconsistancies within a single world view. In this way it helps indicate where Jung is ambivalent within his own structures as well as where he has responded creatively to the gaps in his predecessor's models.

If with Weininger the ego or consciousness was identified with the basic spiritual substance of life, the monad, thereby relegating the unconscious feminine to non-existence, Freud made room for an unconscious of repressed instincts and a feminine configuration based on the missing penis. Jung approaches Freud's imbalance directly when he says that the emphasis on repressed sexuality as the driving force of the id is itself a result of repression. Freud's perception of sexuality structuring the unconscious reflects the fact that the conscious mind is restricted by cultural mores which repress sexuality. In addition Jung himself draws on mathematical symmetry to provide a basis for criticism.

> Three can be regarded as a relative totality... Psychologically, however, three—if the context indicated that it refers to the self—should be understood as a defective quaternity or as a stepping stone towards it.[1]

Thus Freud's triadic model of the psyche constituted by the id, ego and superego can be seen as a stepping stone toward Jung's quadratic system. Regardless of the internal inconsistencies in Jung's schematizations they all have an essential symmetry.

In analysing the terms of the basic encounter of the individual with the world Jung identifies two primary and largely incompatible ways of registering data: one based on sensation as a function of the conscious mind. Thus an individual either perceives data with the senses or grasps the implications of the situation with the intuition. What makes one an attribute of the conscious mind and the other an attribute of the unconscious seems to be a function of cultural values. Jung saw the distinction as a function of the degree to which will could come into play, consciousness again (as with Weininger and Freud) being associated with capacity for willful control, which implies that the will is both a cultural value and the implement by which other values are realized such as Weininger's categorical imperative.

A comparable opposition describes how the data is processed, thinking being the "digestive" function of the conscious mind and feeling being that of the unconscious mind.

> For complete orientation all four functions should contribute equally: thinking should facilitate cognition, feeling should tell us how and to what extent a thing is important to us, sensation should convey concrete reality through seeing, hearing, tasting, etc., and intuition should enable us to divine the hidden possibilities in the background.[2]

In practice such a balance is hard to come by.

> Sensation...rules out any simultaneous activity since the latter is not concerned with the present but with a sixth sense of hidden posibilities. In the same way thinking is opposed to feeling since thinking should not be deflected from its purpose by feeling values just as feeling is usually vitiated by too much reflection.[3]

Thus every individual finds one term of each pair more natural for him/her and these form the basis of his characteristic approach to the world. They make up this persona or public face. Once again thinking is more susceptible than feeling to conscious control and so is considered characteristic of the conscious mind.

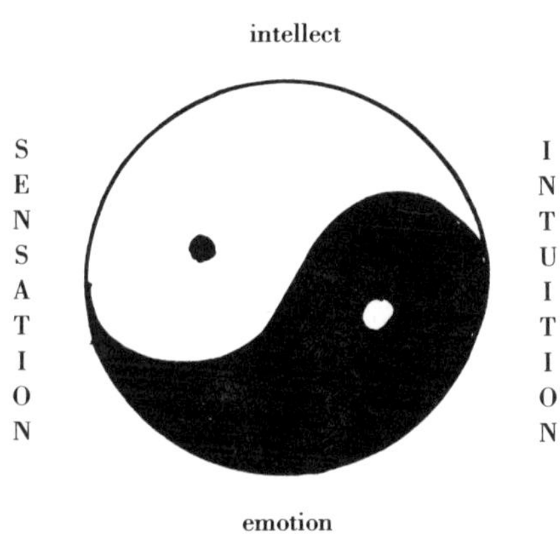

In the West will was the implement by which a male God created the world; willing becomes the crucial act of creativity. On the human plane the individual will becomes the creative agent which through objectivity rather than intuition and logic rather than feeling seeks to manipulate and transform the external world.

Although the conscious mind has almost universally been associated with the masculine, a tradition which Jung continues, the attributes and functions of consciousness in the West have certain special characteristics. Whereas the symmetrical patterns of thought revealed in mandalas, for example,are used in the East for purposes of meditation not practical domination, in the West patterns of thought are applied to the empirical world.

> The processes of science...move by the union of empirical fact and rational thought, in a way which cannot be disentangled. There is in science as in all our lives, a continuous to and fro of factual discovery, then of thought about the implications of what we have discovered, and so back to the facts for testing and discovery.... This union of two methods is the very basis of science. Whitehead...dated the Scientific Revolution from the moment when Galileo and his contemporaries understood that the two methods, the empirical and the logical, are each meaningless alone, and they must be put together.... (O)ur material successes stem from joining to...logic a ruthless appeal, at each bold deductive step, back to the hard empirical facts.[4]

Thus in Jungian terms the scientific mind is the masculine mind characterized by thinking and sensation which has been highly valued by Western culture. As we can see from the symmetrical structure thinking can just as well combine with intuition and feeling with sensation. As we will see later through looking at the *I Ching*, another equally valid system can result from combining thinking and intuition in a cultural context which does not value individual domination of the external world. In such a non-Western context other questions are asked and meaningful conjunctions between self and world are sought elsewhere than in the scientific realm. Within the world of the *I Ching* to ask the same question twice is considered youthful folly

> The young fool takes me.
> At the first oracle I inform him.
> If he asks two or three times, it is importunity.
> If he importunes I give him no information.
> Perseverance furthers.[5]

In the scientific world, however, repeatability is the key to veracity and public presentability. Successful experiments are those which can be done again and again with the same results, those which pose again and again the same question receive the same answer. In neither realm, however, can these meaningful conjunctions be preordained. Einstein when asked about the efficacy of his theories could only say that it is "beautiful" when they "work," when there is a correspondence with reality. Einstein coined the aphorism "As far as the laws of mathematics refer to reality, they are not certain; and as far as they are certain, they do not refer to reality."[6]

In spite of Jung's familiarity with the *I Ching*, in spite of his respect for the principle of synchronicity on which it functions, Jung continues with the traditional conception that the masculine mind is the conscious mind as we think of consciousness and that masculinity has a connection with actual men. He goes on to describe the unconscious elements as combining in the "feminine" mind whose domain is the inner world moving through the "blind dynamism of nature," or that "love which is blind."[7]

Not only does Jung continue the traditional categories of masculine and feminine, but he continues traditional imbalances in what is considered appropriate behavior for each. Although he praises the men who incorporate their feminine qualities and in doing so often create works of art, he criticizes the women who step outside their proper sphere to meddle in matters of the intellect. In doing so they become victims of irrational opinions and are likened to stores of misinformation one might find among old newspaper clippings, sermon fragments and assorted pithy sayings of parents.

At the same time as Jung continues these traditional conceptions his sense of symmetry and balance lead him to create the concepts of *anima* and *animus* which give to the masculine and feminine as well as to men and women a new status of equality. The *anima* represents the feminine as it exists in the masculine mind; the *animus* the masculine aspects of the feminine mind. Falling in love often involves attraction to one's *anima* or *animus* as it is projected outward on a member of the opposite sex. However, since Jung felt that "for complete orientation all four functions should contribute equally,"[8] the task of growth is the incorporation of any individual's opposite into one's life. Thus in spite of the nasty things he said about "animus-possessed" women, in spite of the fact that he continued to talk of the feminine mind as the unconscious mind, he unlike Freud does provide sexually symmetrical concepts for access to "complete" consciousness.

In addition for Jung psychic health depends on a living relationship between the conscious and the unconscious; therefore he focused a great deal of attention on the ways in which the two domains could relate. The role of the archetype is to provide such a link. *Anima* and *animus* as links between the conscious and unconscious function as archetypes.

In so far as they are genderized they lend a degree of ultimacy to the notions of masculine and feminine; in so far as they represent one's inner opposite, whatever its characteristics, they give ultimate status only to a principle of opposition between the conscious and the unconscious.

The ambiguity between *anima* and *animus* as principles of opposition and as opposition between genders is present in much of the material on archetypes. On the one hand Jung talks of them in very specific language with reference to dream images of individuals or mythic images of diverse cultures. It is probably on the basis of such writings that Jungians frequently catalogue archetypes as if they were static and conveniently knowable. For example, one talks about the Demeter archetype or the Persephone archetype in a way that serves to perpetuate a cultural past perhaps in excess of its utility. On the other hand Jung talks of the archetype in the most abstract of terms, as, for example, "a group of symmetry elements" which as an "unmanifest, intelligible factor...orders material facts in a meaningful, regular way."[9] In these terms number is the archetype *par excellence*.[10]

We are all familiar with the conscious and practical significance of number as a way of counting. Jung points out, however, that while numbers on this side of the border are quantities, on the other, they are "autonomus psychic entities capable of making qualitative statements..." Number bridges the polarities between the quantitative and the qualitative, intellect and feeling, conscious and unconscious.

Although Westerners are more familiar with the quantitative aspect of number, zero was a late comer to the world of mathematics probably *because* of its qualitative significance. Less than two thousand years ago, theorists in India integrated it into mathematics and evolved the decimal system, which was transmitted to the West to become the basis of Western computation. Originally the concept of zero was part of the Indian metaphysical system where it symbolized infinity. Thus it began its career as a symbol of unity, as the undifferentiated potentiality from which all life flows. "Zero is to number as potentiality is to actuality" to the Indian mind.[11] As a magic circle or mandala, zero was part of a system of mystical symbols which were not expected to correspond to the empirical world.

Another example of the qualitative interpretation of number emerges in a surprising story told by Marie Louise von Franz at an Eranos lecture in August 1978. Eleven Chinese generals were asked to vote on whether or not to retreat. Three voted to attack, eight voted to retreat; the decision was to attack because three was the number of harmony and therefore indicated the right choice for that moment. In short, other cultures are more familiar with the quantitative use of number than we are in the West where science has dominated our sense of the real.

Jung himself addresses directly the problem of distinguishing between the definition of an archetype and its use, between it as a formative potentiality and as a formed entity.

> With regard to its content, an archetype is only traceable when it is conscious and therefore filled with the material of conscious experience. but its form, as I have elsewhere explained, is somewhat comparable to the axial system of a crystal, which, so to speak, preforms the crystal formation in the mother liquor, without itself possessing a material existence. The latter appears at last in the way that the ions and molecules crystallize. The archetype itself is an empty formal element, a *facultas praeformandi* or an a *priori* given possibility of a form of conception. What is inherited is not a conception but rather a form which in this respect corresponds exactly with the equally formally determined instincts (patterns of behavior). With reference to the definiteness of form, the analogy with crystal formation is likewise enlightening, for there the axial system determines the stereometric structure but not the concrete form of the individual crystal.[12]

The function of the archetype, then, to mediate between the conscious and the unconscious, is apparent in its structure. Like the axes of a crystal which exist by virture of their poles, the archetype is the link between the conscious and the unconscious, the essential oppositions of the psyche. How one clothes the polarities is a function of social and personal history.

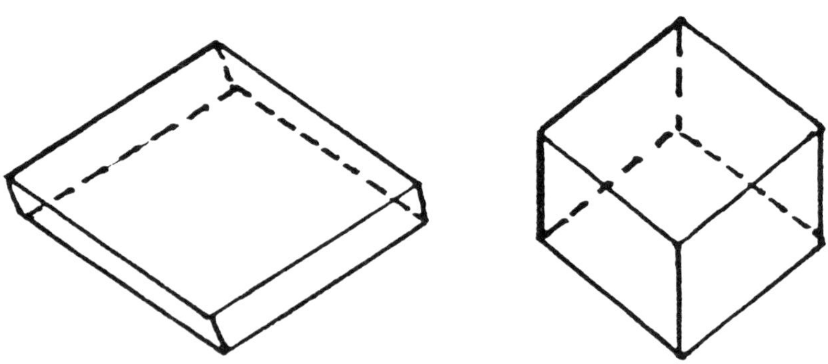

Different habits of calcite crystals

Although personal histories vary considerably, the culture in which one lives determines to some extent the possibilities one can conceive of. Nonetheless there seem to be certain generalities in this profusion of individual and social histories. All cultures seem to define themselves in opposition to their concept of nature; thus they exist by contrast to other cultures and to nature. This is of particular relevance to gender distinctions since men are the culture creators who have established initiation rites by which the young male has access to the cultural reality. Women on the other hand are associated with nature and often specifically with that manifestation of nature as mother from whom the men must differentiate themselves.

Mircea Eliade affirms[13] that men undergo communal cultural initiation rites in which they are dramatically separated from nature and/or unconscious identification with the mother. Women, on the other hand, when they do have such rites, for example at the onset of menstruation, find themselves affirming a continued identity with nature. Whatever rituals men undergo at that time take place in a social context which gives them a new identity within a communal group. Women usually undergo such rituals individually; one effect is to reinforce their place in a social framework identified with their untransformed natures.

The thesis of Sherry Ortner's article "Is Female to Male As Nature Is to Culture?" is that such identification of woman with nature as opposed to culture is a universal phenomenon. First of all woman's physiology appears to be more involved with the "species of life," i.e. with propagating the species.

> Her association with the structurally subordinate domestic context is charged with the crucial function of transforming animal-like infants into cultured beings; "woman's psyche"...appropriately molded to mothering functions by her own socialization...tends toward greater personalism and less mediated modes of relating...[14]

The association of woman with the body physically, with the care of the body socially and with the unconscious psychologically is a universal constant which places woman forever on the margins of society where she is either "below" others as the evil witch, the castrating mother, or above as the mother goddess, the merciful dispenser of salvation.[15] What they never attain is the status of equal individual; what they never use is will power. Freud condemned his mother-in-law for *wanting* in her old age what as matter of course every old *man* wants, which is in its most general terms to be recognized as an individual, an end in oneself capable of self-definition. Will, as we can see from Assagioli's discussion of it, is closely tied to the cultural ideal.

> Motives and intentions are based on evaluations; evaluations are based on the

> *meaning* attributed to life. But this meaning, in its turn, is given by the aim or purpose of life itself, and by its achievement. Therefore it is very helpful for putting the will into operation to have a positive conception of the meaning and purpose of life; to admit, first of all, that life *has* a purpose which is meaningful; second that this purpose is positive, constructive, valuable—in one word, that it is good.[16]

Will then is the way to goodness. Weininger who expressed so blatantly that woman has no consciousness or morality implies that she can have no will which would give access to it. Freud in spite of his elaboration of a psychoanalytic technique permitting personal evolution to both men and women, remained tied to theories which bore the imprint of the moral universe described by Weininger. Although Jung's concept of archetype and respect for symmetry has led to the elaboration of sexually balanced principles of consciousness, the partiality with which he moves into the third dimension still partly retains the bias of Weininger's moral universe.

The self in Jung's scheme is the archetype of wholeness; the most important forms it takes are

> geometrical structures containing elements of the circle and quaternity; namely circular and spherical forms on the one hand, which can be represented either purely geometrically or as objects; and, on the other hand, quadratic figures divided into four or in the form of a cross. They can also be four objects or persons related to one another in meaning or by the way they are arranged.[17]

The first question this invites implies an imbalance which expresses itself in a variety of ways in his various diagrams: why does he move with the circle into the three dimensions of the sphere but not with the square? Or in other words, what elaboration of oppositions would the six faces and eight apexes of the cube invite that he prefers to ignore? We can begin to answer this question by looking at the way in which he arranges the different elements of a quaternity.

Within the quaternity, or square, there is frequently an imbalance reflected in the division of parts into three plus one; three parts of one kind countered by an Other. Jung takes an example from the physical world: the three spatial dimensions in which change occurs versus time. Nonetheless such an example does not take into account the interpenetration of time and space and their mutual relativity.

In cultural terms moving into the fourth dimension or missing Other is a considerable step beyond the tripolar bias of Western conception. Whether we take the Christian trinity of the Father, Son and Holy Ghost or the Freudian triad of id, ego and superego (representing the man-made cultural ideal to which the male ego relates through will) we find there a male bias. In the Trinity as in the Oedipal conflict the main tension is between father and son. The missing part is the feminine whose presence

Jung feels is essential as the Other.[18] Jung rejects an all male quaternity and in doing so affirms the necessity of a feminine element. The all male quaternity of Horus and his three sons "is not aboriginal enough, for it misses the antagonistic feminine element."[19]

Jung would replace the Horus quaternity with that of the alchemist Maier which includes Apollo, Vulcan, Mercurius and Luna.

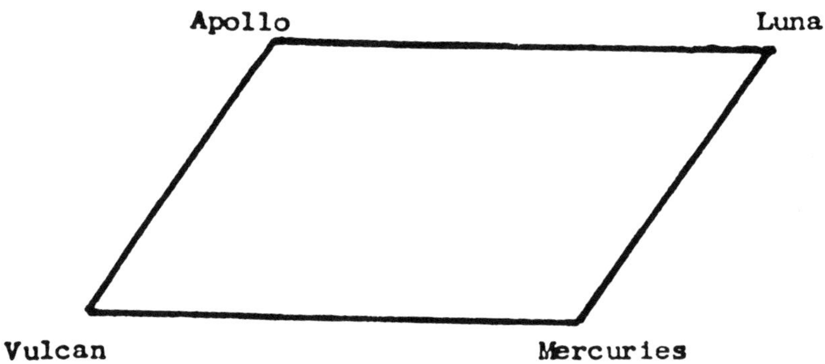

Jung sees the belated Catholic dogma of the assumption of Mary into heaven as a recognition of the missing feminine.[20] If we look at the feminine figures in these quaternities, we will see the same images of women that Sherry Ortner found on the peripheries of all cultures.

In both of these quaternities, the "good" one and the "bad" one, the official one and the subversive one, the Catholic one and the alchemical one, we will see a lack of differentiation. Luna is a dark feminine figure who as the missing factor in an all-male trinity would be the antagonist. Whereas Apollo, Vulcan and Mercurius represent qualities for us, they arrived at these through individualized adventures; their personal names have become symbolic. Luna on the other hand is first of all a symbol, the term for which has become a personal name. The Virgin Mary, on the other hand, is the nurturing mother whose positive fertility has been underlined as the expense of her dark and/or sexual side. Although she has a name, it is qualified by "Virgin," which is essential to her designation.

Comparable imbalances are evident in Jung's work itself. For example, he describes the human figures which can represent the self:

> a god, a prince, a great man, an historical personality, a dearly loved father, an admired example, the successful older brother—in short a figure that transcends the ego personality of the dreamer. There are corresponding feminine figures in a woman's psychology.[21]

His sense of symmetry leads him to hint at categories he does not elaborate. He leaves these comparable feminine figures slighted in much the way he does the concept of *animus*. Jung approaches the problem of the *animus* in the following words:

> Since the *anima* is an archetype that is found in men, it is reasonable to assume that an equivalent archetype must be present in women; for just as the man is compensated by a feminine element, so woman is compensated by a masculine one...the *animus* corresponds to the paternal Logos just as the *anima* corresponds to the maternal Eros.[22]

Whereas freedom from projection comes to men through experiencing the *anima* as mother, lover, daughter, seductress, etc., such freedom is more difficult for women who are limited to father-figure *animuses*. Lacking their own developed discrimination, *animus*-possessed women ingest the father-*animus*,"the sum of conventional opinion" only to display a

> vast number of commonplaces, misapplied truisms,cliches from newspapers and novels, shop-soiled platitudes of every description interspersed with vulgar abuse and brainsplitting lack of logic.[23]

Nonetheless Jung has opened the way for a new dimension of equilibrium simply through the creation of theoretically balanced categories.

If Jung's cultural bias compromises the balance implicit in the concepts of *anima* and *animus*, at least he went beyond Freud's male-only Oedipus complex by giving to both sexes a consciousness-creating principle. For Jung the "projection-making factor"[24] is crucial to consciousness since it calls into form the unconscious which can then be integrated into consciousness. Projection-making then is the first step toward consciousness creating, a step that the unconscious makes but which can be encouraged by the consciousness. The work of the conscious mind follows by separating the projected material from "reality." In men this projection-making factor is the *anima* which

> possesses all the outstanding characteristics of a feminine being. She is not the invention of the conscious but a spontaneous product of the unconscious.[25]

In the case of the young man the *anima* is identical with the mother-figure, which projection can only be dissolved

> when the son sees that in the realm of his psyche there is an image not only of the mother but of the daughter, the sister, the beloved, the heavenly goddess, and the chthonic Baubo. Every mother and every beloved is forced to become the carrier and embodiment of the omnipresent and ageless image which corresponds to the deepest reality in man.[26]

While Jung himself paid much more attention to the man's *anima* than to the woman's *animus*, his wife began to fill the gap. For the woman, according to Emma Jung, the appearance of the *animus* reflects to some extent the role of men in the society. Whereas the *anima* commonly appears as a woman having a definite relationship to the man, the woman's *animus* "appears either as a plurality of men, as a group of fathers, a council, a court or some other gathering of wise men..."[27] Since the social order has surrounded women with many men in positions of authority, *animus* images retain this plurality and impersonal authority, which can give them the feeling of being external and overpowering. Such cultural biases are perpetuated by Jung in statements that the Wise Old Man is the archetype of meaning while the *anima* is the archetype of life.[28] The *animus* then is the vehicle of culture while the *anima* is that of nature. While women are urged to incorporate the personal *animus* by creating "a place for it in her life and personality" and initiating "some undertaking with the energy belonging to it,"[29] the *animus* as supra-personal entity can never be subordinated to her conscious mind.[30] The *animus* retains the aura of father as distinguished from the son; the *anima* on the other hand evolves out of the mother-figure into many feminine beings who lose the aura of authority. The *animus* gives the meaning whereas the *anima* gives the image,[31] which still depends on the former for significance.

Although in order to be talked about, the *anima* and *animus* must take on specific contents which reflect a specific society,they are nonetheless terms which permit one to make observations about women in terms comparable to those made about men. While Emma Jung's discussions of the *animus* and *anima* reflect the society in which she grew up, they also point out ways in which women can develop, with the asymmetries indicating the areas where something new should be sought. In terms of the cube the *animus* as Wise Old Man is differentiated along all three axes: in terms of morality he is good, in terms of age he is old and in terms of gender he is male. Access to these categories gives the man an advantage over the woman who in so far as she remains undifferentiated also remains dependent on those around her with whom her identity is diffused. In so far as a woman's identity depends on that of her father, husband or son, she herself is dependent on them. Women, for example, do not become sages, they serve sages in hope of sharing their aura.

The problem of this lack of differentiation for women is dramatized in the myth of Demeter and Persephone, the mother and daughter whose separation brings on winter's barrenness. Hades, who as Persephone's husband becomes a kind of son-in-law to Demeter, does not go to her to ask for Persephone as his wife but goes over her head to Zeus who advises him to lure her away with a trap. Demeter expresses her powerlessness in relation to her abducted daughter by placing the curse of barrenness on the earth. Zeus to save the earth orders Hades to return Persephone and works out a compromise between demands of Hades and those of Demeter: each shall have Persephone half the time. Persephone, however, has little to say about her own fate. Zeus, king of the gods, clearly has the power and collaborates with Hades as with another less powerful individual; Demeter has only the power to thwart the greening of the earth and is in no way differentiated sufficiently from Persephone to collaborate with her as a separate individual. For the earth to flourish mother and daughter are joined. The mother distinguishes herself from Persephone through her anger and her power over the earth; however, Hades and Zeus treat them both alike in so far as neither engages the women as conscious individuals capable of intent and choice.

Zeus and Hades are both potential *animus* images. The former is certainly the Wise Old Man figure and the latter is what Emma Jung describes as a "lightning change artist who can assume any form and makes extensive use of this ability.[32] Jung himself links these two figures by seeing the trickster personality as the negative (and therefore slighted) aspect of the wise old man:[33] he acts like Hades, who used a flower to spring the trap on Persephone; he is linked to the natural world. The trickster Hades relates to Persephone as a sexual being; the mother Demeter relates to Persephone through their shared fertility. Both are defined in terms of their bodies, however, just as in Weininger's world-view where the prostitute was desired for the pleasure of her sexuality and the mother for the fertility of hers. Neither had access to the world of consciousness.

Although Jung creates the terms *animus* and *anima*, their use is different. Although an integrated *animus* may give to woman a "capacity for reflection, deliberation and self-knowledge,"[34] nonetheless it is easier for her to remain *animus* possessed

> wrapped in a veil of illusions by her demon-familiar, and, as the daughter who alone understands her father,...she is translated to the land of sheep, where she is put to graze by the shepherd of her soul, the *animus*.[35]

The *anima*-possessed man, however, is at the hands of

> the great illusionist, the seductress, who draws him into life with her Maya...Because she is his greatest danger she demands from a man his greatest, and if he has it in him she will receive it.[36]

The cultural bias which has permitted men to relate to a variety of women has also been the stage for the many works of art and belles lettres where men have represented their "Lady Soul." In women on the other hand the development of Logos, "often only a regrettable accident,"[37] is not encouraged any more than is personal contact with a variety of men.

Animus-loaded father-figures continue to use women as body for the transmission of their meanings even if they are only shop-worn platitudes. Although *animus* exists as well as *anima*, the former puts women out to pasture while the latter brings out the deepest and most essential reality for men. Thus although more equitable than either Freud or Weininger, Jung shares their cultural bias.

A comparable slanting surfaces in his choice of conceptual frameworks. Whereas he moves freely between two and three dimensions when talking of circles and spheres, quadratic figures are never extended into their three-dimensional expression, the cube. Jung approaches this extension when he uses the axial arrangement of crystalline structure as a metaphor for archetypes. He also projects archetype as a container, a room, but he then shifts his attention to the person inside, who always happens to be a male symbol for the self.

> The inhabitation of the quadratic space leads to the human figure. Apart from the geometrical and arithmetical symbols, this is the commonest figure for the self. It is either a god or a godlike human being, a prince, priest, a great man, an historical personality, the successful elder brother—in short, a figure that transcends the ego personality of the dreamer.[38]

When Jung moves explicitly into three dimensions, he uses a pyramid structure which retains the relationship he established between room and occupant, between the four and the one, the oppositions and their resolutions in an ideal.

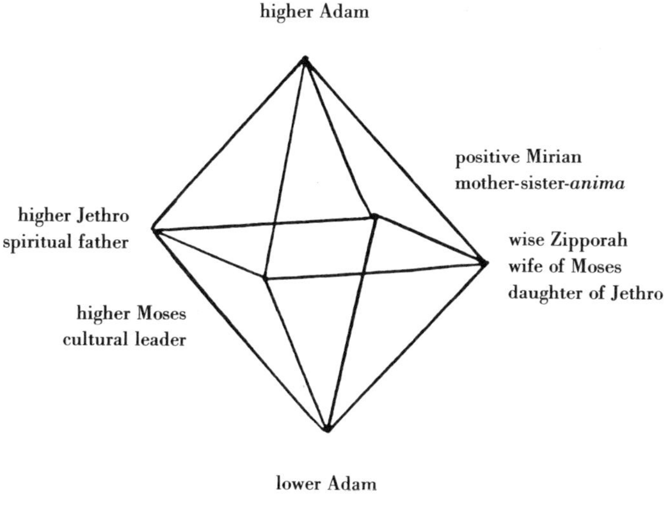

Jung explores this form through his analysis of the Moses quaternity.[39] Here we have in fact a double pyramid with the Lower Adam at the bottom. His evolution moves through two sets of oppositions represented by Moses as culture hero or law-giver and his wife Zipporah who is also the daughter of Jethro, the inner guide or spiritual father, and who is paired with Miriam the higher mother. At the top of the upper pyramid is the higher Adam or anthropos. Thus the central evolving figures are all male: lower Adam becomes higher Adam through the intermediaries of Moses as culture hero and Jethro as inner hero to whom the female figures relate as daughter, wife and mother. The importance of the pairing becomes evident in terms of the Shadow Quaternio in which Zipporah, the link between Moses and Jethro, is replaced by the Ethiopian Woman who is both nameless and black and who leads the movement downward to the serpent from the lower Adam. The serpent as cold-blooded creature represents the loss of the psychic rapport which is possible among warm-blooded creatures. However, it

> seems to possess a peculiar wisdom of its own and a knowledge that is often thought to be supernatural...this is the treasure which the snake guards, and also the reason why the snake signifies evil and darkness on the one hand and wisdom on the other.[40]

The function of the double pyramid form is to diagram the splitting into opposites and hence consciousness of an unconscious entity and their final resolution in terms of an ideal conscious wholeness.

Although Freud became more pessimistic toward the end of his life about the possibility of the unconscious becoming totally "cured" through being made conscious by means of psychoanalysis, Jung took the next step of seeing something irreducible in the unconscious. He sees in the Moses quaternity a counterbalance to the notion of evil as *privatio boni* which has so widened the gap between the conscious and the unconscious that the world is threatened with universal disorientation.[41] Nonetheless the Moses Quaternio retains a certain imbalance. Although the female figures were included in the basic square as the necessary antagonists for the male figures, the addition of the lower and higher Adams creates a uniquely male axis for directional movement. The lower Adam evolves into the higher Adam or descends into the serpent for its wisdom. The women function as antagonists whose significance depends on their impact on the evolution of the male figures. The female figures have taken on the role of embodying the unconscious; although they are differentiated morally in terms of how they effect the male figures, they do not attain full individual status in relation to their own evolution.

Jung saw the dangerous disorientation caused by the gap between the conscious and the unconscious in terms of science. He expressed concern, for example, over the attention paid to matter by modern science and to the reversal of morality evident in the institutionalized cruelty of the last war. Materialism relates to the traditional perception of women, although Jung himself does not pursue this. Such gaps have been approached by his followers.

James Hillman, a contemporary Jungian, in his article "Great Mother and Puer"[42] has elaborated on the materialistic and maternal factor which is implicit in the hero myth and which underlies the formation and evaluation of the male ego, the criterion for consciousness.[43] Freud in canonizing the Oedipus myth formalized the act of killing as the essential act of emerging into consciousness: Oedipus must kill the father *for* the mother thus asserting himself as a conscious individual, something Persophene never accomplished. Translated into contemporary terms the culture hero is distinguished by various conquests, glories, spoils which serve the mother in the form of material civilization. Since the struggle is also against the mother as that *Prima materia* out of which consciousness emerges by making distinctions, the assertive masculinity of the hero is perpetually engaged.

> Unfortunately, however, this heroic deed has no lasting effects. Again and again the hero must renew the struggle, and always under the symbol of deliverance from the mother.... The mother is thus the demon who challenges the hero to his deeds and lays in his path the poisonous serpent that will strike him.[44]

What Hillman adds is that it is also the mother who receives the hero's quarry and bestows the laurels. The female figure retains her power and position as antagonist in so far as she is undifferentiated. In this way the male ego-hero remains bound to her by opposition; he enjoys the elaboration of his distinctions and differences in so far as they contrast with the undifferentiated female figure. This ideal is "the thoroughly analyzed man, sublimated, integrated, whole, conscious,"[45] but through such an ideal "creative spirit and fertile matter are embraced and embattled to the destruction of both."[46]

Jung himself perpetuates this ideal. He arranges a series of double pyramids into a circle through which one moves through the serpent up to the anthropos or ideal of consciousness. One moves from unconsciousness through differentiation to a state of wholeness which is masculine consciousness plus what has been gained by contact with the female antagonist. Such a state of perfect conscious wholeness is necessarily static and the trajectory toward it involves fixed relationships with female figures, whose help or hindrance sends one backward or forward, downward or upward. By claiming that one direction is preferable to another, the pathway toward it is fixed in terms of defined relationships, such as those with the female antagonists. One goal, one ideal, is held above all others. When the male ego identifies with the ideal, which is certainly encouraged by the society, it projects its counterideal on the woman. Whereas the female figures retain their moral charge of good or bad in so far as they help or hinder the evolution of the male figure, the male on the other hand completes his ideal of consciousness by contact with "evil." Wholeness involves moving through the various polarities. The hero can only accomplish his marvelous deeds when there is a dragon to be slain, an unconscious mother figure to differentiate himself from. What is missing is the ordinariness of the individual, the personal case history which provides for the specificity both of the would-be hero and his mother whose assets and defects have influenced his particular shape. But again the problem arises: how can we more fully appreciate or even perceive the details of the case history which is by definition in motion when the concepts for its interpretation are static?

Notes to Chapter 4

1. C.G. Jung, *The Collected Works of C.G. Jung*, ed. Sir Herbert Read, Michael Fordham and Gerhard Adler, trans. R.F.C. Hull (New York: Pantheon Books, Bollingen Series XX, 1959), vol. 9, part II, p. 224. All further references to the complete works of Jung will be as follows: name of author, volume number, page number.
2. Jung, vol. 6, p. 518.
3. Jung, vol. 6, pp. 553-4
4. J. Bronowski, *The Common Sense of Science* (Cambridge: Harvard University Press, 1961), p. 30 as cited in Jean Y. Matlack, "A Life Study of A Psycho-therapist: Marjorie Murray Burtt," Diss. Univ. of Massachusetts 1976, p. 5.
5. *The I Ching*, trans. Richard Wilhelm and Cary F. Baynes, 3rd ed. (Princeton: Princeton University Press, Bollingen Series XIX, 1967), p. 21.
6. Fritjof Capra, *The Tao of Physics* (Boulder: Shambhala, 1975), p. 41.
7. Jung, vol. 10, p. 132.
8. Jung, vol. 6, p. 518
9. Jung, vol. 9, part II, p. 224.
10. Jung, vol. 10, p. 409.
11. A.K. Coomaraswamy, "Kha and Other Words Denoting Zero in Connection with The Metaphysics of Space," *Bulletin of the School of Oriental Studies*, London Institution, Part 3, 1934, p. 496 as cited in Joanna Macy, "Perfection of Wisdom: Mother of All Buddas," *Anima*, vol. 3, No. 1 (1977), p. 77.
12. Jung, vol. 9, part II, p. 224.
13. Mircea Eliade, *Rites and Symbols of Initiation* (New York: Harper & Row, 1958), p.47.
14. Sherry B. Ortner, "Is Female to Male As Nature to Culture?" in *Woman Culture and Society*, ed. Michelle Zimbalist Rosaldo and Louise Lamphere (Stanford: Stanford University Press, 1974), p. 84.

15. Ortner, p. 86.
16. Roberto Assagioli, *The Act of Will* (London: Wildwood House, 1973), p. 141.
17. Jung, vol. 9, part II, p. 224.
18. Jung, vol. 9, part II, p. 243.
19. Jung, vol. 9, part II, p. 243.
20. Jung, "Psychological Approaches to The Dogma of The Trinity," vol.11.
21. Jung, vol. 9, part II, p. 225.
22. Jung, vol. 9, part II, p. 14.
23. Jung, vol. 9, part II, p. 15.
24. Jung, vol. 9, part II, pp.12.
25. Jung, vol. 9, part II, pp. 13-4.
26. Jung, vol. 9, part II, pp. 12-3.
27. Emma Jung, *Animus and Anima* (Zurich: Spring Publications, 1957), p. 27.
28. Emma Jung, p. 80.
29. Emma Jung, p. 39.
30. Emma Jung, p. 39.
31. Emma Jung, p. 26.
32. Emma Jung, p. 27.
33. Jung, vol. 9, part I, p. 374.
34. Jung, vol. 9, part II, p. 16.
35. Jung, vol. 9, part II, p. 16.
36. Jung, vol. 9, part II, p. 13.
37. Jung, vol. 9, part II, pp. 14.
38. Jung, vol. 9, part II, p. 225.
39. Jung, vol. 9, part II, pp. 226-7.
40. Jung, vol. 9, part II, p. 234.
41. Jung, vol. 9, part II, p. 269.
42. Hillman, "The Great Mother, Her Son, Her Hero, and The Puer."
43. Hillman, p. 104.
44. Jung, vol. 5, p. 580.
45. Hillman, p. 104.
46. Hillman, p. 104.

5
The Cube

Although Jung moved into three dimensions through the double or single pyramid, he maintained a directional bias toward an ideal of wholeness. Evolutionary progress toward it was made through women in fixed relationships serving as foils to the male consciousness. Jung himself describes the quaternity as a natural sorting device. "It is a system of coordinates that is used almost instinctively for dividing up and arranging a chaotic multiplicity."[1] Only a strong cultural bias could have prevented him from an equally instinctive use of the cube, especially given his concern for symmetry which guarantees the needed balance between the conscious and the unconscious, the higher being and the shadow.

By taking the cube as a model, one is obliged to consider the implications of the poles located at the ends of each of the three axes. Retaining woman as antagonist to a differentiated male pattern is not sufficient. Woman can no longer be an undifferentiated foil to masculine consciousness, the missing fourth in a quaternity. The cube necessitates that she be further differentiated: young or old, good or bad. The cube creates a theoretical framework which provides more space for the specificity of the individual woman. In addition the cube implies no directional movement, hence no preference is given to evolution along a male or any other axis.

The earlier cultural preferences given to the father-son relationship by Freud, Jung and Christianity in general is reflected in the male axis having direction in their models. The differentiation of the son from the father is crucial to Freudian psychology and its successors. Hence Oedipus killing the father becomes the typical act of discrimination necessary for the establishment of the son's own consciousness and individuality, as distinct from inherited conceptions. The unity of the mother-daughter relationship is reflected in the stasis of the feminine figures. Change and evolution are inherent in the configuration of the male figures.

Moreover one has only to look again at Freud's canonization of the Oedipus myth to see in it an acceptance of what had been primary evil, the murder of one's father, the differentiation of self from society. Although for Sophocles the act of murder carried with it such guilt that Oedipus had to stab out his eyes, his "I," for Freud the important fact lay in the need for the act of murder to establish the new consciousness. Freud's ideal that psychoanalysis could so strengthen the ego that it would become independent of the superego, would also include the demise of guilt which binds one to the past. As Jung exanded considerably the notion of the unconscious, new images for differentiation were made. Yet an encounter with "evil" was still built into the act of becoming conscious. Woman, the antagonist, was given space in the cosmology although not elaborated.

To better see what is missing in these earlier conceptions we can first look at the male face of the cube and then compare it to the female one.

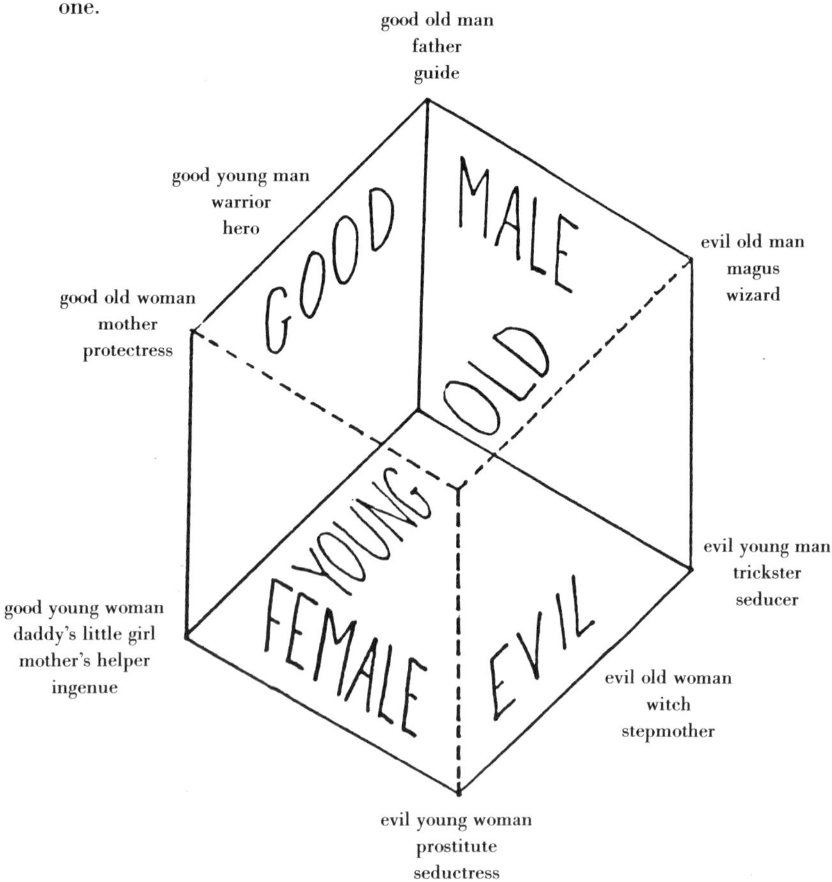

good old man
father
guide

bad old man
magus
wizard

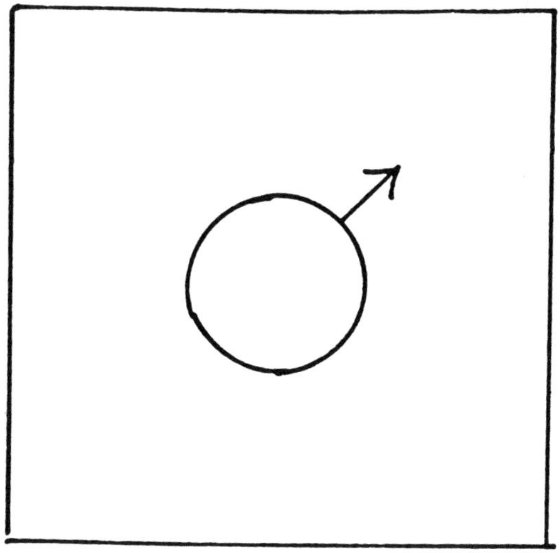

good young man
hero
warrior

bad young man
trickster
politician

good old woman
mother
protectress

bad old woman
witch
stepmother

good young woman
daddy's little girl
mother's helper
ngenue

bad young woman
prostitute
seductress

Since there are three axes to the cube, there are six faces as well as eight apexes. One can separate out any one face of the cube which permits one to compare it to its opposite and to see any imbalances which result from the comparison or from the distribution of figures on the four corners.

Whereas the *senex* is the wise old man who is the archetype of meaning, the bearer of goodness and wisdom in and of himself, the mother is first of all fertility which becomes significant in terms of its use through another's meaning. She can be extended to include matter and include all the goods for which men perform their heroics, their quest for power, honor, glory and the love of women. This limitation of the good mother image becomes more and more obvious as it is applied to women beyond their childbearing years. In contrast the meaning of the *senex* can continue well into his old age.

As we saw in terms of the evolution of the male consciousness on the pyramid, men evolve through some contact with "evil." The blurring of the boundary between good and evil for men has been gradually taking place in Western literature over the last two hundred years.[2] Whereas the figure of the confidence man was satanic to Milton, in *The Magus* of John Fowles he emerges as a god-like figure. In Melville's book *The Confidence Man* the impossibility of distinguishing between the evil man and the good man is clearly presented. Such ambiguity is already present in the Biblical tale of the Fall. The apple brought evil into the world as well as knowledge which has worked good. In a comparable way Jung includes a trickster element in the wise old man. The witch on the other hand has had no redeeming qualities and was traditionally not included in a concept of the good old woman although she represents the other side of the unrealistic expectations of the mother.

> We look for the wonderful woman to be our salvation, which then constellates the other side, betrayal and destruction... The expectation to be saved by a woman goes hand in hand with the fear of being destroyed by a woman.[3]

Once the medical profession coopted the healing capacities of the medieval witch, few redeeming qualities were left to her.[4]

The *puer aeternus*, the good young man, distinguishes himself from the *senex* by an arrogance which "reflects his cocky narcissistic conviction that he is about his father's business, a child of the spirit, bearing its message."[5] He refuses any ties but embarks on "an odyssey of the spirit, a wandering that never comes home to any hearth or city."[6] By refusing heroics for the sake of the mother/matter, he seeks to be the free spirit. The good young girl however is as we saw with Demeter and Persephone closely tied to the mother. "The mother *is* the daughter," to borrow the words of Anne Sexton, and both serve the man as daughter-wife-mother-*anima*.

The trickster figure, or the bad young man, is also linked in Jung's concepts to the wise old man as a necessary although neglected and to some extent negligible underside. He is described as "an ambiguous elfin character," a dwarf-figure, "a naturalistic vegetation-numen sprung from the underworld."[7] The bad young woman, the prostitute, however, has no redeeming connections with the good mother. Although like the witch she had spiritual significance in the ancient world as a temple prostitute, such redeeming characteristics have been denied her in modern society where she is a commodity so stigmatized morally that the possibility of change is practically denied her.[8]

What in fact characterizes the differences between the "good" and the "bad" surfaces of the cube is a function of role. The good figures are true to their role definitions, whereas the bad figures are in some way shape-shifters.The magus or wizard is traditionally one who can play with appearances, and especially those which differentiate moral categories. The magus is he who through the appearance of evil can work good and vice versa.[9] Such a magus figure long before Melville and Fowles was legendary throughout Germany. He is described as an old man who lived in a mysterious house, the gate obstinately shut against the curious, where the noise of his powerful furnace could be heard, evidence of his efforts to transmute base metals to gold. Often he lived with an innocent daughter who knew nothing of her father's activities. The trickster figure can dissociate himself physically. In the Trickster myth of the Winnebago Indians, Trickster's right arm fights his left, he burns his anus and eats his own intestines, and his penis becomes detached from his body.[10] The witch can traditionally assume many shapes, especially those of animals such as the black cat which bode evil; and the prostitute's job is to assume the form and character desired by her client's fantasies for which she is a projection screen. As shape-shifters these figures are often the instruments of change and transformation in others and hence threaten the stability of traditional roles defining the good mother, father, son and daughter; women traditionally have less access to change and growth.

Although all of the "bad" figures share certain characteristics, sexual differences persist. The female shape-shifters are oriented toward others: the witch seeks power of influence over others, the prostitute assumes appearances pleasing to others. This gender difference becomes more evident when we try to distinguish the characteristics that separate the old from the young.

The simplest and most evident difference due to age has to do with one's relation to the future. The young with the future before them think of the goals they wish to accomplish. The old with the future behind them think more in terms of teaching, helping or guiding others. When this is applied to men and women, however, there are differences according to gender. Women are in fact almost always expected to live their lives in terms of others

> In her own right, a woman is nothing, for her total existence is bound up in being *for* someone rather than in being someone![11]

This feminine characteristic goes back to the whole range of symbols, myths and artifacts from which Neumann attempts in *The Great Mother* to extract some essential quality. He concludes that her basic characteristic is that of being the vessel which is known only by what it contains. True to his Western bias, he sees the feminine as nothing in and of itself. This assumption becomes important in relation to the problem of aging. Whereas a man having lived an honorable and fruitful life may turn in his old age to share the fruits of his labor with others, he nonetheless expects to be an end in himself![12] A woman on the other hand is always expected to live for and through others. "As a mother she ought to be content to know that her three children are fairly happy, and she ought to sacrifice her wishes to their needs."[13] There is no specific place in a woman's life for living for herself, for self-definition, neither in youth nor in age. Thus living for herself is in fact a secondary characteristic of "bad" women: the prostitute accumulates personal power in the form of money and the witch is feared because she has occult power over others and can shift her shape to execute her wishes.

Similarly only in terms of the woman is sexually pleasurable activity separated from fertility. For a man many offspring is a sign of virility which includes both sexual prowess and sexual potency. For the woman, however, the ideal is the virgin mother. For fertile matter/mother to rest quietly in opposition to the creative spirit, sexual activity must be removed from it. Furthermore the union sought in the orgasm which women are only recently actively claiming blurs ego boundaries and role identities. In this way sexual activity is itself a form of shape-shifting. Since culture is largely man-made, role defining and shape mediating are activities men are familiar with. Men then as the creators reserve for themselves the perogatives of changing under certain circumstances. Women as objects defined by men in terms of their roles relating to men are denied access to transformation.

Once again there is an overlay with the good and bad axis. While fertility is the mark of the mother and potential fertility that of the daughter, sexual activity as the perogative of the prostitute serves the consciousness of the client, that of the witch serves herself and/or the devil. The witch's traditional activity, riding a broomstick, can be symbolic of the masturbatory activities she was habitually suspected of. Preparatory to making nightly trips she would supposedly grease a rod and place it between her thighs.[14] In some traditions intercourse with the devil was necessary to her identity.[15] Elsewhere she is associated with the goat, a pan-like figure for sexual activity.[16] Since sexual activity which serves the individual woman is mixed with that which serves the devil, one sees once again the identity of woman as evil, and above all woman's sexual activity. Even the sexual activity of delivery is described in monstrous terms by that champion of the gentle delivery, Leboyer.

> An intransigent force—wild, out of control—has gripped the infant.... The prison has gone berserk, demanding its prisoner's death...this monstrous unremitting pressure that is crushing the baby, pushing it out toward the world—and this blind wall, which is holding it back, confining it—These things are all one: the mother.[17]

Using the cube as an ideal mathematical model we first sought the symmetry which resulted from the differentiation of the three axes: gender, age morality. Once the gender axis was separated by Jung from that of the morality axis, the cube functioned to indicate those poles where gender differentiation was incomplete. Now that we have filled in the apexes of the cube, sexual imbalances are still present in the language we have at our disposal to describe and identify the figures who inhabit each apex. Our vocabulary, like our concepts have been influenced by our Western habit of mind that sees good and evil as mutually exclusive and that then bases the pattern for other oppositions on that model. A first step toward encouraging evolution and change equally for both men and women would be to find or create a degenderized vocabulary.[18] Then the cube encourages a full appreciation of both poles of each axis: evil is not just an absence of good, nor is the feminine only lack of the masculine, nor age the waning of youth. When each pole can assume its own identity and function then we can fully appreciate opposition as necessary gradation on continua, against the mathematical perfection of the cube any interpretive skew will become evident.

Notes to Chapter 5

1. Jung, vol. 9, part II, p. 242.
2. See John G. Blair, *The Confidence Man in Modern Fiction* (London: Vision Press, 1979).

3. Hillman, p. 114.
4. Barbara Ehrenreich and Deirdre English, "Witches, Midwives and Nurses," *Glass Mountain Pamphlet* No. 1.
5. Hillman, p. 114.
6. Hillman, p. 108.
7. Jung, vol. 9, part I, p. 374.
8. Temple prostitution was an institution rite for the women who through intercourse with a stranger or priest felt they encountered God. "Through such an experience the woman comes into possession of her own masculine soul, which is then no longer projected entirely outside herself into a man who has for her the value of a god, with godlike authority. Thus she has become complete, whole."
   M. Esther Harding, *Woman's Mysteries* (New York: Bantam Books, 1973), p. 221.
9. See John G. Blair, *The Confidence Man in Modern Fiction*, Grillot de Givry, *Witchcraft, Magic and Alchemy* (New York: Houghton Mifflin, 1931), p. 53.
10. Michael W. Whan, "'Don Juan,' Trickster," *Spring 1978*, p. 23.
11. Rita Gross, "On Being A Religious Jewish Woman," *Anima*, vol. 1, No. 1, (Fall Equinox 1974), p. 24.
12. Ellman, p. 132.
13. *The Letters of Sigmund Freud*, p. 38 as cited in Ellman, p. 132.
14. Grillot de Givry, p. 70.
15. Grillot de Givry, pp. 58-9.

6
Motion: Perls

Such a degenderized vocabulary emerges in Gestalt psychology where specific individual contexts provide the framing device rather than traditional concepts. The focus is on the dynamic relationship between context and subject.

In 1912 Max Wertheimer[1] published a paper that has been considered the beginning of Gestalt. In it he considered the phenomenon that flashes of light appearing at intervals of less that 3/100 of a second seem to the observer as continuous. From this observation he came to describe perceived experience as an emergent experience which is dependent on both the stimuli and their interrelationship. Both neural organization and perceptual experience spring into existence as an entire field arises from the interrelationships of the total input and not from an additive combination of external elements which affect one's senses. From here the psychological goal was to open a more flexible and unified conception of the relationship between the individual and the environment.

Instead of a static concept against which to measure the world, man and his environment are seen in terms of a dynamic and on-going relationship. Implicit in this position is the Heisenberg uncertainity principle which asserts that the observer has an impact on the observation. The additive conception of reality which leads to a single conclusion has been replaced by an elastic one based on the tension between the elements in a given interaction. Thus a Jungian ideal of the "thoroughly analyzed man, sublimated, integrated, whole, conscious,"[2] would be one who included in his psyche a balance between all of the four Jungian faculties. A comparable Gestalt ideal might be seen as the person who was sufficiently adaptable to find in herself or himself what every given situation called for.

Fritz Perls has enjoyed making Gestalt psychology known. While rejecting the title "founder of Gestalt" he accepts being called the refinder of Gestalt Therapy?[3] He sees the "law of Gestalt formation" as that by which the world maintains itself. The making of a Gestalt or state of wholeness is an organic function through which a need emerges and finds its completion or satisfaction, the condition of having done enough. (Satisfaction derives from *satis*, the Latin for "enough," and *facere*, the Latin for "make" or "do"). In seeking a basis which is organic and biological, Gestalt therapy tries to return to an understanding of the human organism more basic than the cultural images of what s/he ought to be.

Since Perls is impatient with concepts and considers the intellect to be the whore of true intelligence, he uses categories sparingly. Nonetheless those he uses function to restore balance between the opposite poles of the gender and morality axes.

Whereas Freud focused on the superego as locus of cultural ideals, he did not concern himself with what any ideal projects as its negative counterpart. Repressed instincts do not take into account negative cultural images such as those projected on women which are as essential to maintaining the positive image as repressed instincts. Perls, however, addresses directly this lack by talking of an infraego as well as a superego. Moreover he demystifies them by calling them generally the "two clowns" or specifically "topdog" and "underdog," recalling to some extent Eric Berne's Parent and Child.

> The topdog usually is righteous and authoritarian; he knows best. He is sometimes right, but always righteous. The topdog is a bully, and works with "You should" and "You should not."...The underdog manipulates with being defensive, apologetic, wheedling, playing the cry-baby, and such.[4]

Although Jung took seriously the negative underpinning of any ideal, he shared Freud's differential evaluation of the ideal. Jung's wise old man has a relationship to the trickster figure, but the two are not given parity. The latter is looked down on as valueless or meaningless in comparison to the former as the very archetype of meaning. Perls by his choice of language permits us to look at both with equal interest and attention. There is no implicit value judgement.

Acculturation is also evident in the problem of projection as considered by Freud and Jung. Whereas the former used the masculine model of the Oedipus complex for both sexes, Jung developed the concepts of *animus* and *anima*. When dealing with the images of the self, Jung again used genderized terms and assumed that the self or ego-transcending ideal would always be of the same sex as the ego-bearer, leaving women with fewer role models. Perls too sees projection as a function of one's self-images, or Jung's *persona*, but his focus is so aimed at dynamic movement that rather than conceptualize the "negative" of one's image he lets there be an energy field which can be approached openly and creatively. Whereas Freud and Jung let cultural concepts fix ego boundaries, Perls is interested in the area where individual and environment intersect actively.

> But in living organisims, the ego boundary has to be negotiated by us because there is something outside that is needed.[5]

The ego boundary is involved in defining both the inner space and the outer space where one must seek the satisfaction and closure of inner needs. By being concerned with process rather than concepts, Perls focuses on the energy field within which the "I" contacts the "other" as the locus of movement and growth.

This juncture is the place where Gestalts are being created. There are two other concepts important to this process: background and foreground, which implicitly evoke a three-dimensional frame of reference. Into the foreground emerges whatever need is most pressing, whatever is the "emergency. It presents its demands until there is satisfaction, until the need has been fulfilled and closure can occur, until the wound can heal. Since we are all full of unfinished business, the most urgent is that which relates most directly to survival. When that one is cared for, the next in intensity will emerge.

Supported only by the structure of background/foreground, Gestalt therapy is for Perls the one existential therapy which does not have recourse to borrowed concepts. Besides existentialism Perls recognizes two basic types of philosophy: "aboutism" in which one remains in the realm of concepts and talks about the situation while failing to do anything about it; and "shouldism" which expects ideals of behavior to have an impact on the world and how people behave. Only his existentialism deals with the here and now; all the others borrow concepts which limit their openness to the present. "Buber takes from Judaism, Tillich from Protestantism, Sartre from Socialism, Heidegger from language, Binswanger from psychoanalysis, and so on."[7]. For Perls anarchy replaces hierarchy and awareness *per se* replaces any conceptualized ideal or "cured" condition. Taking Heisenberg's uncertainty principle with great confidence, Perls believes that awareness is curative, that observation does in fact change the observed condition.[8] If the organism can be freed from the cultural baggage of conceptualized shoulds and other restraints which impede its own self-regulatory functioning, it can find what it needs to heal itself. Awareness of this self-regulatory mechanism is all that is needed in order to have the confidence to trust oneself.

Balance, which he like Jung values, is a state of flexibility rather than a concept of psychic completion. For a fruitful balance to exist background and foreground must be readily interchangeable.[9] In addition three-dimensional ambidexterity is another indication of balance in the individual. All parts of the body must relate easily, the right and the left, the front and the back, the upper part and the lower part. Perls claimed he could see in a person's body all he needed to know about his or her history.

By valuing dynamic balance in the person rather than static completion of cultural ideals, Perls has accepted personal responsibility for sexism. Rather than projecting definitions of masculine and feminine which would reflect his personal and cultural bias, he has instead looked at his own sexuality. For example, he admits to being less tolerant of dependency and weakness in men, as in himself, and to enjoying proximity to the opposite sex. He likes manipulating women sexually and spoke of one woman whom he had too much respect for to see sexually. He also relates these tendencies to his own attitudes to homosexuality.[10] Having criticized Freud for institutionalizing in the tries to keep his theories and techniques as free as possible from his personal imbalances or voids.

The presence of such gaps or holes, sterile voids, is one way of talking about the neurotic:[11]

> One neurotic has no eyes, many have no ears, others no heart or memory or legs to stand on. Most neurotic people have no center. The function of the therapist is as a projection screen for the missing part so that it can be brought to awareness and mobilized in oneself.[12]

What keeps the neurotic in the state of avoidance based on the gaps Perls calls catastrophic expectations. The typology of catastrophe points toward what comes after the end; such are topdog's scripts saying "If you do this or that, you will die, you will not be loved, the world will end." Or the catastrophic situation could be conceived as follows: one is caught in an escalating pattern, let's say of anger, which suddenly collapses to panic. If one's topdog or ego ideals value the assertiveness of anger but condemn the withdrawal of panic then the sudden feeling of change is complicated by a negative judgement. The cure then is twofold: first of all to project on the therapist and/or the group one's missing part, then to identify with the projection and be critically aware of the therapist and audience so that one can "Wake up from the trance of catastrophic expectations."[13] To this one could add "Wake up from the catastrophic illusion that opposites are 'linked' by a void rather than by gradations on a continuum." By returning to the cube we have a framework within which catastrophes can be contained by means of gradation and of a frame to counterbalance judgement.

Perls describes a woman who could not let go of her daughter: by reliving the birth of the daughter with her Perls led her to see the sterile void she had where others had personality and uniqueness. By helping the woman face this situation the void became fertile with her own substance and worthiness. The question "What are you avoiding?" is one of the key questions which is also crucial to dreamwork.[14]

The dream is first of all a complement to the day's activities and reality. In addition it can be treated so as to maximize its capacity to respond to the void. Perls suggests that the dream not be analyzed, but relived as if it were happening now. Instead of catagorizing the different elements in terms, for example, of *anima* and *animus*, Perls suggests you take all the parts yourself. Thus as one subjectifies dream images one begins to integrate them into oneself, which is quite different from the tendency to objectify one's inner sexual opposite almost as if it were a member of the opposite sex complete with the usual cultural prejudices. After sorting out all the different parts of a dream, one can begin to play with them and reassemble them as if they were parts of a puzzle. Perls suggests playing out encounters between different parts of the dream. If you choose sensitive opposites and write a script for their encounter, they will start fighting each other thereby creating

> the eternal conflict, game, the self-torture game. As the process goes on there is a mutual learning until we come to an understanding, and an appreciation of differences, until we come to a oneness and integration of opposing forces. Then the civil war is finished, and your energies are ready for your struggles with the world.[15]

Such dreamwork is a "kind of central attack right into the midst of your non-existence."[16] In a comparable perspective Perls has had people assume the role of different parts of their bodies as well as minds and dramatize encounters between them. His aim is to bring to life all the rejected and denied aspects of a person. Without any categories which call attention to sexual or moral distinctions, Perls invites everyone to incorporate all of their missing pieces and in so doing reclaim the powers they have projected upon the world. His basis is in emotional satisfaction rather than in interpretive theories. The question he does not address is the need for intellectually perceivable order.

Traditional analysis, by contrast, invites one to establish an analytical distance from one's dreams and other projected material; traditional social values encourage one to remain in a state of projecting on authority figures and those who supposedly represent higher levels of being. Roberto Assagioli, for example, who sees the goal of psychological work to be the synthesis of the psyche to a transcendent level of awareness, says that those who cannot attain such an elevated state themselves should remain dependent upon others, the receivers of their projections.[17] Rather than awareness as a cure, he sees the will to transcend as the needed link between the individual and the ideal—shades of Weininger.

Traditionally changes were seen in a religious framework such as Assagioli perpetuates. Life had the goal of realizing a higher state whatever the terms a given society used to define it. Assagioli gives a simplified version of this in his diagrams for conflict resolution: any pair of opposites can be resolved by moving to a higher plane.[18]

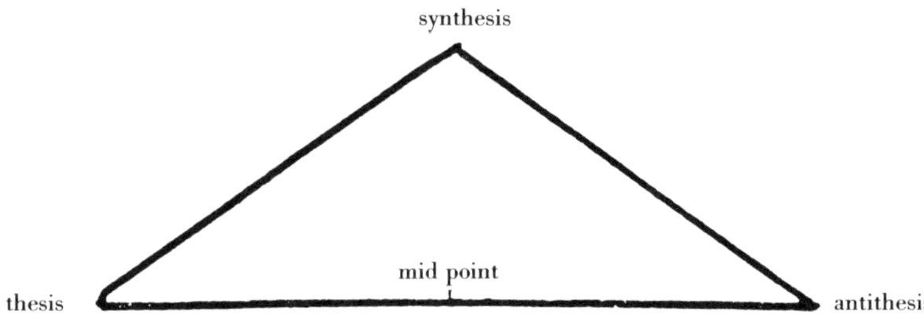

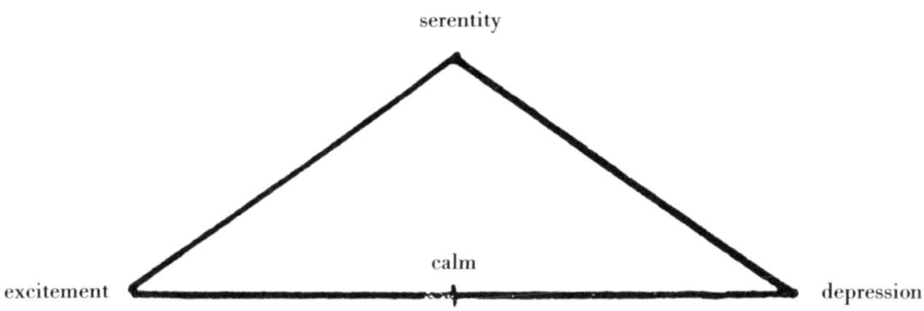

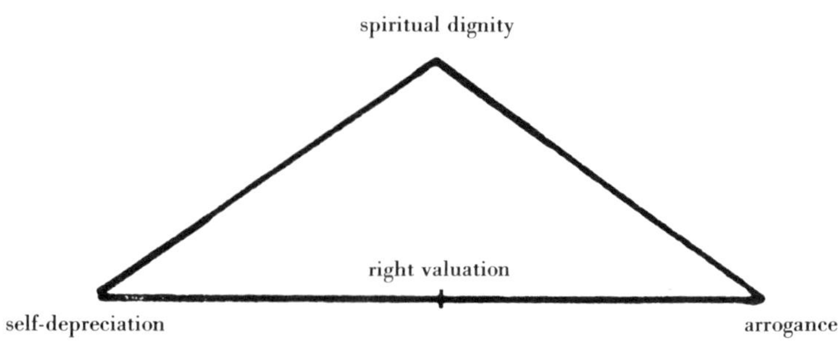

Act of Will, 102

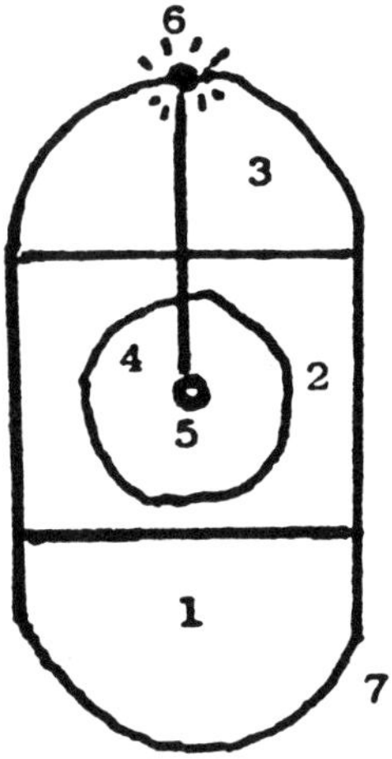

1. lower unconscious
2. middle unconscious
3. higher unconscious
   or superconscious includes
   ethical imperations
4. the field of consciousness
5. the conscious self or I
6. the higher self
7. the collective unconscious

Psychosynthesis, 17

Perls understanding of times of change can be seen as analogous to conflicts between old states of being and what is emerging. In traditional societies rituals created passages between the different stages marked out in the given conception of reality. The major periods of one's life were marked by ritual observances: entry into the age of consciousness, entry into the social world, puberty, marriage, death.

> Every ritual process has three stages: the first is the separation from the previous social reality; the second is the liminal or transitional stage, a sacred period between the other two stages; and the third is the constitution of a new order and perception of reality.[19]

Though traditional cultures in which ritual still functions differ from ours which is in the process of rapid and open-ended change, Gestalt therapy still focuses on that liminal stage, an open energy field polarized by conflicting pulls backward and forward. In a traditional society there were accepted standards which described each stage of a person's life: certain activities and attitudes were appropriate at different times to members of different sexes and different social and age groups. In spite of his modernity and eclecticism Assagioli retains some of the essential traditional structures: the figure of the wise old man represents a higher state of being; masculine and feminine still serve as basic terms for describing various polarities in life?[20] Today, however, there is such a variety of cultural norms with little concern for apparent appropriateness that renovating traditional heirarchies with their implicit teleology begs the challenge of living today?[21] Although Assagioli was willing to admit that there are many personae relevant to a given individual, in contrast to Jung's emphasis on a *persona*, he dealt with them in terms of ascending the ladder of consciousness. Identification of the subpersonalities which impeded one from accomplishing what s/he wanted is a step toward freeing the will which can then seek to realize the ideal as it is relevant to one's stage of evolution.

Perls confronts directly the field of transformation. Instead of seeing fixed stages which must be passed through at appropriate times, Perls relies on an individual's sense of being stuck, of being in a frame of mind which is out of touch with the situation which must be lived in. The outcome, the new perception of reality, is up to the individual to create. Although we can learn from initiation rites, they cannot have the same function for us because unlike the communities where they were indigenous, we have no standard into which we are initiating people and no sure knowledge of where they are coming from or going to. Once one has perceived oneself as a potential script writer, one must create alternatives to the traditional scenarios which are in fact like individuals in the process of change.

Nonetheless the intermediate stage, the liminal energy field remains crucial.

> The attributes of liminality or of the liminal *personae* (threshold people) are necessarily ambiguous, since this condition and these persons elude or slip through the network of classification that normally locate states and positions in cultural space. Liminal entities are neither here nor there; they are betwixt and between...[22]

A sense of energized, almost sacred, space is already present in the circle in which Perls has a group sit. The person needing help is in the center where s/he can receive intensified energy. In relation to this person Perls would act as or catalyze the liminal figure. First of all as projection screen, the stability of Perls "identity" is compromised. Second by focusing on the gaps in the person's character the taken-for-granted everyday reality is no longer maintained. Third what Perls asks of the person further destructures ordinary "reality." Talking to parts of oneself, assuming all the parts of a dream recall the demands made by Don Juan on Castenada. The master-trickster asked his student to learn about plants, treating them first of all as anthropological data, but then talking to them. Castenada says, "I went as far as kneeling in front of the plant but I could not bring myself to speak to it. I felt ridiculous."[23] Similarly one can feel ridiculous talking to parts of oneself, taking oneself apart as Trickster did in the Winnebago myth cited earlier. However by lessening one's sense of identity and importance, a basis of humility and receptivity is established which permits greater openness to the unknown.

Important liminal figures include all of the inhabitants of the "bad" side of the cube: the shape-shifting witch, the client-accommodating prostitute, the morally ambiguous magus, as well as the self-dissociative trickster. Whereas traditional societies alloted places for these figures, ours does not, especially concerning women. The witch used to be a healer whose knowledge of the natural world of herbs was a resource. The prostitute used to be a priestess who used sexual union as an image for union with the godhead. In our society, however, these figures are scorned, limiting the role possibilities for women who have been objectified in terms of their relationships to men.

Once liminal encounters take place outside of a traditional setting, certain potential problems emerge. Whereas social norms in a traditional society determine what issues are involved with any given ritual, more than one gestalt can emerge.

> If more than one gestalt emerges, a split, a dichotomy, an inner conflict might develop, weakening the potential that has to be invested to complete the unfinished situation.[24]

Confronted with this situation the individual begins to "decide" and with no guidelines can end up in the self-torture game of indecisiveness. On the other hand this state might at times correspond to what Perls describes as his schizophrenic layer.

> I contacted a layer of fractionalized, scattered bits and pieces, like tiny introjects, foreign material. Many were physical sensations and pictures, but unconnected.[25]

Once accepted, contact with this layer permitted a change to emerge in Perls' sexual habits: "The leching compulsion got a real break."[26] The former religious frameworks of traditional societies provided hierarchies on the basis of which to make choices and usually a concept of the universe which could transcend and encompass moments of falling apart. Without tradition what is a frame which can help us through such times?

Another threat to the smooth functioning of the natural flow of gestalt formation and satisfaction is rigidity of background and foreground differentiation. "Every interference with the elasticity of foreground/background interchange brings about neurotic or psychotic phenomena."[27] Such rigidity relates to the catastrophe scripts to which our cultural biases are prone. As long as evil is the absence of good, falling into it can be falling out of the real world. With reality thingified and objectified through concepts, falling apart can be a catastrophe. If nothing is only no-thing, then encountering nothing is annihilation, catastrophe. With recognition the sterile void becomes the fertile void out of which the new may emerge. Or in terms of the cube it is the exploration of poles needed for continua and balance to emerge. Such a concept moves us beyond what Jung was doing when he admitted the female antagonist into the structure of the psyche. We must admit age and evil as they interrelate and combine with gender differences.

Perls has been influenced by his time in a Zen monastery and his assumption that foreground and background can have a flexible relationship presupposes a world view in which opposites are not considered mutually exclusive. Yin and Yang are interrelated in just this way, as interchangeable foreground and background. Their symmetry is one of movement and interchange rather than of balanced mirror-image opposition based on a static arrangement of parts. When he criticizes Freud for being a "placer" of people in spite of his concern for the case history, he is criticizing the whole Western bias. Similarly "hypnosis"[28] or the threat of becoming stuck through identifying our categories and concepts with reality reflects this bias.

> It is an artificial attitude that makes sections in the stream of change, and calls them things.... When we shall know the truth of things we shall realize how absurd it is for us to worship isolated products of the incessant series of transformations as though they were eternal and real. Life is no thing or state of a thing, but a continuous movement or change.[29]

Perls wishes to bring us to an awareness of this state of change and of the artificiality of our concepts. By using such a sparse vocabulary as topdog and underdog, foreground and background he has created empty vessels into which anything can be put depending on the person and the situation. We are invited by his terms to attend to the processes of change. For this purpose they serve even better than the oriental terms yin and yang which have become associated with our notions of feminine and masculine. In addition his theories also invite an awareness of "I" and in this sense veer away from the Zen idea of no-mind.The opening and closing of gestalts in the flow of life presumes the presence of the ego; one is always somebody aware of something.

Although the cube may seem like the most static of symmetries, it has other possibilities which Perls' vocabulary invites. Although each of the apexes represent a character type or configuration of age, gender and morality which has social resonance, seeing them as foreground and background to one another invites moving the cube in addition to moving gradually between the cubes poles. By superimposing the terms of Perls on the cube we can take a new perspective on the polar oppositions our heritage has encouraged us to keep discrete. Any one of the apexes can relate to its opposite as foreground to background encouraging an inclusive rather than an exclusive perspective on oppositions. Relating to these different configurations is made easier by such a flexible framework which frees the "I" from a fixed attachment to any one apex, any one identity. One could go a step farther ideologically and see "foreground" as the projection of an energy knot for which background serves as field.

A comparison of the tendencies in Eastern and Western visual arts can serve as an analogy for what is different in the orientation to the world. The eye can be metaphor for the "I."

Through the science of optics in the West the eye has been treated as an inanimate object.

> The optical result was the development of linear perspective: the single vanishing point and the penetration of landscape by a single piercing eye, my eye, my dominating eye.[30]

The guided line could now penetrate infinity just as rows of trees lead your eye down a symmetrical road, implying that there is just one correct place to stand, from which to view the world. This could be another image for the whole person. Everything in such a world is in a precise and static relation to everything else including infinity, the vanishing point and the viewer, the vantage point.

The Eastern world provides useful contrasts. For example, the eye is in constant motion when reading a Chinese scroll. Should the viewer try to maintain a stable and "perfect" vantage point, the scroll will seem to contain many contradictions: people have different sizes in relation to one another and to the landscape, pieces of landscape have no clear interrelation. Objects do not recede from the viewer, they move toward him/her. There are many parallel perspectives which keep the viewer at an angle to the scene and never the focus of it. There is no fixed center from which to dominate the scene rather the spectator is part of the scene which reveals itself to him/her gradually as s/he moves through it. Although all art is a fixation of reality, Chinese art reminds one of the constant motion of life.

Similarly although the cube is a fixation of reality, also by putting it in motion new dimensions are opened up. It can be thrown like a die and open its world to chance and change. Motion by means of the cube can take one into a fourth dimension.

An anonymous article, "Four-Dimensional Space" uses a moving cube to generate *a* fourth dimension, a time-space called four-dimensional space.

> A straight line, by moving in any direction not in its own length, generates an area; if this area moves in any direction not in its own plane it generates a solid;...in order to get a thing of higher dimensions, we must have motion in a new dimension. But, as the idea of motion is only applicable in space of three dimensions, we must replace it by another which is applicable in our fourth dimensions of time. Such an idea is that of successive existence. We must, therefore, conceive that there is a new three-dimensional space for each successive instant of time; and, by picturing to ourselves the aggregate formed by the successive positions in time-space of a given solid during a given time, we shall get the idea of a four-dimensional solid, which may be called a sur-solid.[31]

Examples of such sur-solids include a person picturing the aggregate of the forms s/he has taken from birth to present or a cube moving in space creating a new dimension through the successive positions taken by its eight apexes, plus its initial and final positions.

> We are to conceive of the cube, and the whole of the three-dimensional space in which it is situated, as floating away in time-space for a given time; the cube will then have an initial and final position, and these will be the end boundaries of the sur-solid. It will therefore have sixteen points.... The successive positions of each of the eight points of the cube will form what may be called a time-line; and adding to these the twenty-four edges of the initial and final cubes, we see that the sur-solid has thirty-two lines.[32]

The details of the new dimension or sur-solid created can be investigated by those interested. What is of most interest in this context is that the sur-solid cannot rest in space but must be seen as a cube moving in "space."

Although Perls provided a totally degenderized vocabulary which is a great step forward, he could not evolve any sense of order within the change, any patterns of change which could in fact make it less threatening. Just as Chinese visual arts presumes change, so language presumes change but change within a patterned context. In the Chinese ideogram, for example, meaning is so implicit that sense depends on context such that reading and writing can only be learned through many years of personal instruction by a teacher. It opens up a world best penetrated by an educated intuition and a sensitivity to the specific and continually changing contexts in which the word can occur.

Just as the visual arts and language of the Chinese incorporate change, so does one of their oldest religious books, the *I Ching*, or *The Book of Changes*. The basic principle here is the flow of energy between the polar opposites of yin and yang which at bottom are empty vessels, as are foreground and background, into which anything can be put. However as particular expressions of the principle of energy flow there are eight trigrams which go to make up the sixty-four hexagrams which represent the archetypal patterns constantly being formed, dissolved and reformed. Such definition marks off the boundary between one pattern and another.

By assigning a name to the moment, meaning is given to the flow of experience. This stopping the flow of experience to observe it and relate it to other moments which parallel or oppose it is also essential to the construction of self awareness and integrity.

Notes to Chapter 6

1. *Encyclopedia Britannica*, Micropedia, vol. IV. (Chicago, London, Toronto, Geneva, Sydney, Tokyo, Manila, Seoul, Johannesburg: Helen Hemingway Benton, Publisher, 1973-74,) p. 512.
2. Hillman, p. 104.
3. Frederick S. Perls, *Gestalt Therapy Verbatim* (New York: Bantam Books, 1971), p. 16
4. Perls, *Gestalt*, p. 19.
5. Perls, *Gestalt*, p. 18.
6. Perls, *Gestalt*, p. 17.
7. Perls, *Gestalt*, p. 17.
8. Frederick S. Perls, *In and Out The Garbage Pail* (New York: Bantam Books, 1972), p. 93.
9. Perls, *Garbage Pail*, p.93.
10. Perls, *Garbage Pail*, p. 240.
11. Perls, *Garbage Pail*, p. 140.
12. Perls, *Gestalt*, p. 40.
13. Perls, *Garbage Pail*, p. 214.
14. Perls, *Garbage Pail*, p. 294.
15. Perls, *Gestalt*, p. 74.
16. Perls, *Gestalt*, p. 75.
17. Roberto Assagioli, *Psychosynthesis* (London: Turnstone Books, 1975), p. 25
18. Assagioli, *The Act of Will*, p. 103.
19. Whan, p. 18.
20. Assagioli, *The Act of Will*, p. 250.
21. Although Assagioli was willing to admit that there are many *personae* relevant to a given individual, in contrast to Jung's emphasis on a *persona*, he dealt with them in terms of asending the ladder of consciousness. Identification of the subpersonalities which impeded one from accomplishing what s/he wanted is a step toward freeing the will which can then seek to realize the ideal as it is relevant to one's stage of evolution.
22. Whan, p. 18.
23. Whan, p. 18.
24. Perls, *Garbage Pail*, p. 92.
25. Perls, *Garbage Pail*, p. 241.
26. Perls, *Garbage Pail*, p. 241.
27. Perls, *Garbage Pail*, p. 93.
28. Perls, *Gestalt*, p. 34.
29. Capra, p. 278.
30. Jacqueline Tyrwhitt, "The Moving Eye," in *Explorations in Communication* (Boston: Beacon Press, 1972), p. 92.
31. Franklin, p. 355.
32. Franklin, p. 355.

7
The Cube In Motion: The *I Ching*

The *I Ching*, the only book to have escaped burning in 460 BC in China, dates back to the legendary ruler Fu Hsi whose dates are located somewhere between 3000 and 4000 B.C. Myth has it that he was sitting by the banks of the Yellow River contemplating cosmogeny and cosmology when a yellow tortoise appeared with the eight trigrams on its back. Through these trigrams Fu Hsi saw the meaning the relationship of heaven to earth expressed in terms of the primordial pair, yin and yang. Yin and yang are so interrelated that there is no sense of one existing without the other, yet yin and yang, despite popular misconceptions, are not the same as feminine and masculine.

The most common way to consult the *I Ching* is to throw three coins, the symbolism of which is relevant here.

cloud
yang

ruler's name
yin

One side of each coin had scrolls on it thought to represent clouds,the other had the name of a ruler. The side with the clouds represented the yang force, the side with the ruler represented the yin force although the rulers were men. Thus there was from the start separation in principle between the yin or feminine force and actual women and between the yang or masculine force and actual men. Yin is represented by a broken line, it is the conditioned, the receptive, and yang is represented by the straight line, the conditioner, the creative. Each trigram is made up of these two basic lines of forces arranged in all possible combinations of three. These eight trigrams were in ancient China thought to represent all the possible situations which could emerge in heaven or earth.

King Wen in 1150 BC was the first to record what had previously been transmitted only orally; he was also the first to double the trigrams producing the 64 hexagrams which now make up the *I Ching*. Like an ideogram each trigram or hexagram presents an image in which many meanings can be found depending on the situation, the time, the place and the person consulting the *I Ching*. Each trigram and hexagram has a structure and a name; the morphology of the structure and of the form of the ideogram carry meaning.

Character:	roots;	translation:	pronunciation:
	sun no sun	change, ease	I

Character:	roots;	translation:	pronunciation:
	water regulation	book	Ching

The ideograms[2] which give the title of the book can provide an example of the way in which their structure also is meaningful. That which represents the "I" in *I Ching* is made up of an ideogram in which there is a symbol of the sun over a symbol of no sun; it means change and ease. "Ching" is made up of two parts one of which means classical book and the other the movement of water as well as of day and night, sun and no sun. In a variety of ways the central principle is reiterated: life is flux.

There are ways in which the ideograms provide perspectives not included in the translations. For example, at the beginning of Chapter IV of "The Great Treatise" it says "The 'Book of Changes' contains the measure of heaven and earth; therefore it enables us to comprehend the tao of heaven and its order."[3] In the Chinese the three characters at the end say "earth, between heaven and the tides." The tides measure the relationship between heaven and earth, since the movement of the water is affected by the moon and the sun and its movements are measurable against the earth's surfaces.

The use of six for the changing yin line and nine for the changing yang line derives from the ancient methods of measuring tides at the equinoxes. In addition six plus nine make fifteen which was the day of the full moon in the Chinese month. The tradition of reading the lines of a hexagram from bottom up also relates to the measurement of the depth of water as in tides and waves, which is also from the bottom up. The importance of the fifth line in any hexagram comes from the movement of a wave which reaches its most forceful thrust just before it breaks at the top. In short the movement of the water is the informing principle of the book.[4] Just as the water is in continual motion, so each hexagram usually contains moving lines which indicate the direction of evolution. Through these lines one hexagram changes into another; in addition further operations on these will indicate the "seed" situation from which the first one arose and a further stage in its evolution.[5]

The eight trigrams originally thought to represent archetypes for all possible situations can be arranged on the eight apexes of a cube. Doing so can permit us to take a new perspective on our own psychic space. First of all elaborating the polarities of each axis in terms which develop from our own cultural heritage provides a familiar starting point. Then by placing the trigrams of the *I Ching* on the apexes as well we can apply the process and perspective of that Oriental world to our own. In this way we can perhaps relate to the *I Ching* more meaningfully and to our own imagery more dynamically and flexibly. Whereas the terminology of the *I Ching* is often specific to Chinese culture and obscure to us, the attitude toward it is relevant to us. Whereas our terminology is familiar to us, we are often limited by a bias toward static concepts.

For example, within our world view it is difficult to see a creative relationship between the mother and the prostitute, who only a few years ago could hardly be mentioned in polite company. By seeing them in terms of trigrams we can see relationships. On the other hand the relational specificities of the trigrams in Chinese cannot mean the same thing to us. The trigram "Sun" is associated with the first daughter for whom there are no special roles in our society. In ancient China on the other hand she was the "socializer" of the family and fulfilled a role similar to the mother in Western culture. Our understanding of the hexagram, then, must be selective rather than blind.

The perspective afforded by the *I Ching* offers a helpful corrective to certain Western habits of mind that have already shown up in the way the cube functions as a conceptual device. As we have seen, one of the properties of a symmetrical mathematical model is to call attention to gaps; by hypothesizing a complete world we can more easily see where the actual one is skewed. Our attitude toward "gaps," however, is affected by our attitude toward the gap as evil, as what Perls called the sterile void, or "nothing" in the catastrophic sense. The Western assumption tends to be that the existance of a gap means that there is something wrong with the structure or with the perceiver. The *I Ching*, on the other hand, sees void as an energy field, an essential fundament which allows creative transformation to take place; the yin without which no yang can emerge.

Water and its perpetual motion remains a key metaphor for the structuring principle of the *I Ching*, a metaphor which suggests new perspectives on the void, which is a recurring theme in Chinese philosophy. Lao Tzu's classic insights illustrate this perspective:

> We put thirty spokes together and call it a wheel; But it is in the spaces where there is nothing that the usefulness of the wheel depends. We turn clay to make a vessel; But it is in the space where there is nothing that the usefulness of the vessel depends. We pierce doors and windows to make a house; And it is in these spaces where there is nothing that the usefulness of the house depends. Therefore just as we take advantage of what is, we should recognize the usefulness of what is not.[6]

Empty spaces in a context which makes them frightening become in Perls' terms sterile voids; those same spaces can become the receptacles through which heaven and earth interrelate through the movement of water. In a world where there is no thing that is absolute, chaos is not absolute either.

In an analogous way the *I Ching* helps to overcome a Western tendency to absolutizing, or taking literally the polar oppositions Jung and many other thinkers have isolated for study. In the use of the cube as a conceptual framework, for example, one danger is that we may assign oppositions to various apexes and then harden them into absolutes which are not only mutually exclusive but also static. Where a Western perspective might see the inhabitants of each apex as a permanent resident, the *I Ching* reminds us that corners are more profoundly conceived as way stations for transients. Movement is perpetual as indeed it is in life. Either the cube or its "residents" move continuously.

In addition the structure, patterns of broken and unbroken lines, also indicate ways of moving on. Whereas the mind's capacity for yes-and-no answers often traps one in the biases of one's culture and its concepts of good and bad, the *I Ching* takes this binary system and treats it symbolically. As such it becomes an empty vessel into which any content can be put without compromising the structure and functioning of the vessel. We are confronted by the form of our thought and freed from its conditioned contents. The specific content is less relevant than how one moves from one way station to the next. To move from Ch'ien, made up of all yang lines to Kun, made up of all yin lines, all of the lines must change, but they can be changed in different sequences which would indicate different paths of moving in the same direction. In addition when at one of the poles one can be sure of feeling the pull of the polar opposite. This is not incompatible with Jung's thinking that healing dream imagery often took the form of one's opposite: the wise old man coming to the young girl, for example. Nor is it incompatible with Perls' call for flexibility between foreground and background, since polar opposites create the deepest foreground/background relationship.

Since every thought can have an opposite, thought presents the possibility of negation. That the cat is white or not white does not call into question the existence of the cat or of color. Images, whether of dream, fantasy or reality do not carry with them negation in the same way that thought does. If the mind moves by opposition, life moves by images. The *I Ching* combines the patterns of thought with the changing reality of images. For example, although one may receive the same hexagram two or more times in response to different questions, that hexagram will not have the same significance because the questioner and the context will not be the same. Similarly any of the figures at the apexes of the cube can have different meanings according to the situation and the person relating to them.

This Hericleitean idea however remains consistent with a linear notion of time as a sequence of events which flows past one. This is a perspective like the one encountered in the visual arts where there is a vantage point and a vanishing point between which one moves. The implicaton is that movement by which time can be measured can continue to infinity. Time as a linear phenomenon undergirds the concepts of cause and effect, the cause being first of all that which precedes effect.

The time concept of the *I Ching* would better correspond to an adage that one cannot step in the same river once since one's presence modifies the river. By framing a question, throwing the coins or the yarrow sticks, one is stepping into the river. What matters in the physical river is a question of density and volume: how much water does one displace. What matters in the psychological world is a matter of intensity: how much energy has been involved in the projection or the question. In ancient China the framing of a question for the *I Ching* used to be a meditation technique the aim of which was to create as dense a question as possible which should not exceed nine words and should be as close to a Zen *koan* and as emotionally charged as possible. By becoming as dense as possible, the question would have greater specific gravity and displace water differently. Throwing a rock into water creates different wave patterns than does throwing a pebble.

The conception of time here is synchronic rather than causal and linear. It presupposes a correlation between the inner state of a person and the outer configuration of events. Past and present as well as distant and close lose their discreteness and interrelate. One's actions in the present moment would be like pebbles or stones dropped into water; the present would be the point of intersection between the individual and the stream of life. Waves from that intersection would move out in all directions. The nature of the movement is not only horizontal as the rings expand in all directions but also vertical as the waves move the water up an down.

Holography is explained in terms of the same metaphor.

> If you drop two pebbles into a pond, concentric circles, or waves, radiate out from each. When the two sets of waves run into each other, they form an interference pattern. Where the crests of waves meet, they make a wave that is twice as high; if a wave meets a trough, the two will cancel each other out to form a flat patch; if two troughs meet they will make a deeper trough. Light waves produce the same complex mix of interference patterns when they intersect. Like the pebbles in a pond, a laser sends out a beam of light waves in one frequency. When two laser beams meet, they produce an interference pattern of light and dark. If one of the beams is reflected off an object, such as a face, and then strikes a photographic plate, the plate will record the interference patterns, thus storing an image of the face.[7]

Continuing in this metaphor, questioning the *I Ching*, throwing one's pebble-question into the stream of time produces waves which intersect with all the other waves which are there. The question of the frequency of the waves is the crucial one.

> It is mind-boggling. The frequency domain deals with the density of occurences only; time and space are collapsed. Ordinary boundaries of space and time, such as locations of any sort disappear. They are...recreated when transformations into the domain of objects and images occur.[8]

Pribram, who is elaborating this theory, recounts an encounter with Skinner, the behaviorist. While Pribram was delving into the mysteries of brain activity, Skinner maintained that it was to him a "black box," in other words impenetrable, and that he would consider only behavior that could be directly observed. He asked Pribram how he could possibly see the brain as isomorphic to the world around one. What happens in the brain when one imagines someone mowing the grass? Pribram at that time had no answer but now feels

> in a better position to answer Skinner. However, it also entails the view that the world around us is isomorphic to the brain, i.e. that the world is in part, made up of the patterning of wave forms.[9]

The "black box" itself set in motion generates waves and offers a continually changing interplay of foreground and background apexes. Like holography it would be concerned with "the transformations involved in moving from one domain to another,"[10] from one role cluster to another. These analogies help to clarify the non-linear conceptions basic to the *I Ching* which also offer a continually changing interplay of foreground and background points on apexes.

Jung was sympathetic to the notion of synchronicity and found that it most often occurred around areas which were emotionally charged, or important for individuation. One of his favorite examples involved a patient for whom the scarab had become an image for the self; as she was talking about it in his office, a beetle, the closet relative to the scarab which exists in Switzerland, flew in the window and landed on Jung's desk. One of his important disciples, Marie-Louise von Franz, adds that she finds synchronic events in a person's life often coincide with archetypal psychic imagery.[11] Both thereby declare their openness to the temporal perspective appropriate to the *I Ching*. Jung's receptivity to this world was made explicit in the way he approached the problem of writing the English introduction to the Wilhelm edition. Before writing he asked the book how it felt about being presented to the Western minds:

> I have questioned the *I Ching* as one questions a person whom one is about to introduce to friends: one asks whether or not it will be agreeable to him. In

> answer the *I Ching* tells me of its religious significance, of the fact that at present it is unknown and misjudged, of its hope of being restored to a place of honor—this last obviously with a side long glance at my as yet unwritten foreword, and above all at the English translation. This seems a perfectly understandable reaction such as one could expect also from a person in a similar situation.[12]

The specific hexagram that *I Ching* spoke through was that of the "cauldron": it "looks upon itself as a vessel in which sacrificial offerings are brought to the gods, ritual food for their nourishment."[13] The vessel is the "archetypal feminine" the empty receptacle; here however, it has a "self-image" considerably different from that common in the West where the emptiness of the feminine makes her worthless in and of herself, an object for men to fill as they wish. This non-Western vessel is

> a cult utensil serving to provide spiritual nourishment for the unconscious elements or forces ("spiritual agencies") that have been projected as gods—in other words, to give these forces the attention they need to play their part in the life of the individual. Indeed this is the original meaning of the *religio*—a careful observation and taking account of the numinous![14]

Attentiveness is the important factor which carries with it intensity and openness to the transcendent.

The implications of the *I Ching's* self-image as vessel go even further. The patriarchal religion which has been instrumental to elaborating our cultural values has been dominated by the interests of men who have projected their *animas* as their complement, their opposite, their other; in short the feminine values of emotional, intuitive and self-sacrificing love have been the basis of the Western concept of soul. However as we have moved farther from the crucifixion of Christ which lies at the origin of this Judeo-Christian conception, we also move farther from the emotional intensity which was surely there at the beginning. Rather it has become an ideal thoroughly embedded in the imbalances of the traditional Western world view from which women suffer more than

Freedom from a genderized vocabulary giv s women more freedom to be human beings, particularly because they have more at stake in changing. Having been defined by their traditional roles for many centuries and having lost access to feminine threshold figures such as witches and prostitutes, women feel stuck. Therefore they have perhaps more emotional energy to invest in the process of change. They also have the present challenge of self-definition which is without cultural precedent for women.

The *I Ching* helps by codifying insights already implicit in focusing on psychic dynamism and in the ongoing drama suggested by the cube in motion. One's self-image is not at the center of the world; in fact, the *I Ching* in places says "It is not I that is posing the question."[15] In addition the absence of pronouns in Chinese reveals a worldview which focuses on the flow of life rather than on its separation into objects and subjects. It is considered best not to call attention to oneself but to frame a question in terms of whether or not an activity or a decision is in accord with the tao. Similarly Perls, while he encourages the use of the "I" does so in a way that breaks down rigid self-images. In playing the different parts of one's dreams or one's body or one's fantasies, "I" must include in one's identity male and female, young and old, good and bad. In this perspective I would rather see Jung's four facilities as possibilities to which I can have access when I need them, rather than components of a static though balanced state of wholeness.

In contrast to the idea of the whole, the importance in the *I Ching* of the "hole," the emptiness, the receptacle, the gap, is present in the functioning of the book as well as in its "self-image." In discussing the trigrams Richard Wilhelm remarks:

> Suprahuman intelligence has from the beginning made use of three mediums of expression—man, animals and plants, in each of which life pulsates in a different rhythm. Chance came to be utilized as a fourth medium; the very absence of an immediate meaning in chance permitted a deeper meaning to come to expression in it.[16]

Thus chance, the absence of predictability, comes to represent the unknown and to provide a means by which deeper meanings can manifest themselves. The *I Ching*, by its incorporation of constant change, perpetual transformation, as Wilhelm suggests, helps to keep Western conceptions, such as those associated here with the cube, from becoming static, from getting stuck.

Wilhelm's evocation of plant, animal and human realms of life helps to further connect the *I Ching* to the conceptual world of the cube, a step which is essential to appreciating the significance of chance motion as the fourth dimension the *I Ching* brings to the West.

The significance of this fourth dimension emerges more clearly once we have seen how the first three dimensions can involve connections between the *I Ching* and the conceptual world of the cube, a process which Wilhelm facilitates with his evocation of the three realms of plant, animal and human. In terms of the evolution of life through more and more complex stages through the human,we can see how the three axes of the cube emerged one at a time. Plants exist through time remaining in one place and reproducing with an androgynous flexibility; animals have locomotion often motivated by desire or sexuality. Only after evolution produces humanity do we find a third dimension based on cultural distinctions which assign values to problems of morality. Animals show not only gender differentiation but begin to show evidence of concern with age. Humans alone are fully occupied in all three dimensions, or in cubal terms, only humans are so complex as to need triangulation of age, gender and morality to try and pin down their identity. A comparable evolution took place in the psychological models from Weininger through Jung. Weininger's world was one dimensional giving reality only to the masculine whose perpetuation through time was synonymous with good; Freud then made sexual motivation the primary driving force in his world, which was still dominated by a sense of the masculine as good; Jung finally differentiated gender differences from moral differences: the good and bad axis became separable from the masculine and feminine one. Perls then added the dimension of change which is essential to human life. Only it has need of the *I Ching*'s fourth dimensional world where the unpredictables and unknown coexist with concepts making the necessary tools of self-understanding mobile and alive rather than rigid and life-denying. Intellect can unite with intuition rather than only with sensation.

To understand the contribution of the *I Ching* it is essential to relate its trigrams to the eight apexes of the cube, a process which is not difficult once we relate the three lines of each trigram to the three axes of the cube: age, sex, and morality. Each line, depending on one's throw of the *I Ching*, may turn out either broken or straight, responding respectively to the forces of ''disintegration'' or ''integration''. Such terminology liberates us from the cultural prejudices attached even to yin and yang, which, despite their relative emptiness as terms, nonetheless carry connotations of feminine and masculine, notions defined differently in China and in the West. In any case, such terms leave us bound to a world of cultural conditioning. In my preferred terms the forces of integration, the straight line, would be associated with the male, the young, and the good on their three respective axes of age, gender, and morality. On these same axes the old, the female, and the bad would correspond to the broken line, the forces of disintegration.

One can protest any of these associations and even the fact of making them.[7] Women and the feminine have elements of integration just as age can permit kinds of psychological integration to take place and evil can be seen as the conditioner of good in some cases. Perhaps these tendencies should be seen as the necessary presence of the opposite within any given force. It is this presence which permits broken lines to change to straight and vice versa. When the straight line moves, its direction is outward toward disintegration; when the broken line moves, its direction is inward, toward integration. Such changes are the basis of the transformation of one configuration—trigram or hexagram—into another.

The fourth element of chance enters when the coins are thrown giving the precise arrangement of broken and straight lines.[18] Like dream imagery or repressed material used creatively, this element of the unknown can invite one to identify with any given category or combination of categories regardless of where one's primary self-image is located in terms of age, gender and morality.

Using the terms we have set up—the broken line for the feminine, the old and the bad, the straight line for the masculine, the young and the good, with the sequence of categories falling in that order to correspond with the evolution of the first, second and third dimensions—the following correspondences can be made:

☷ The trigram *K'un*, the "receptive" would correspond to the evil old woman, the witch.

☵ The trigram *K'an*, the "abysmal" or the moon would correspond to the evil old man, the magus, wizard.

☶ The trigram *K'en*, "keeping still" would correspond to the good old woman, the mother.

☴ The trigram *Sun*, the "gentle" would correspond to the good old man, the father.

☰ The trigram *Ch'ien* the "creative" would correspond to the good young man, the warrior.

☲ The trigram *Li*, the "clinging" or the sun would correspond to the good young woman.

☱ The trigram *Tui*, the joyous, would correspond to the evil young man, the trickster, Weininger's politician.

☳ The trigram *Chen*, the arousing, would correspond to the evil young woman, the prostitute.

Originally all of the eight trigrams in the *I Ching* were associated with natural imagery and all but two of the sixty-four hexagrams were similarly conceived of in terms of nature. The only two man-made images, the "cauldron" and "well," were still based on man's basic needs for food and water. Predictably this natural imagery was read out into the social codes of various times when Chinese commentators wrote. In fact one can distinguish the interpretations made under Confucius by their political character. Just as the natural elements were seen as interpenetrating parts of a whole so were the social roles. Individuals within the system were seen in terms of their social role. There is only one mention of a woman who is neither married nor intending to be

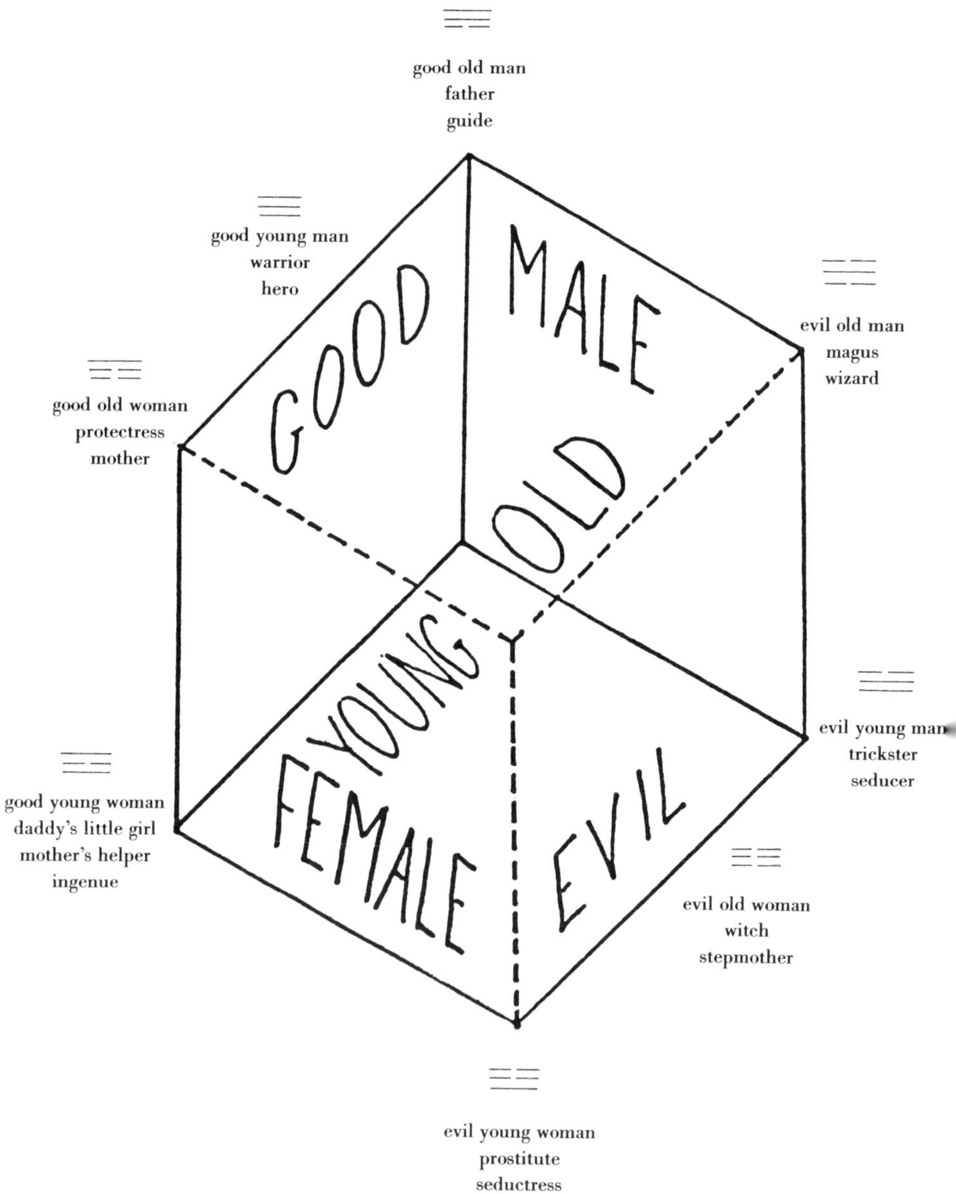
good old man
father
guide
good young man
warrior
hero
good old woman
protectress
mother
evil old man
magus
wizard
evil young man
trickster
seducer
good young woman
daddy's little girl
mother's helper
ingenue
evil old woman
witch
stepmother
evil young woman
prostitute
seductress
GOOD
MALE
OLD
YOUNG
FEMALE
EVIL

married and advice is given not to marry her for she is too strong. Thus women were no less dependent on man than in our society and perhaps a good deal more.

The use of natural phenomena as the basic metaphors of the *I Ching* can both allow it to transcend the arbitrary social categories of its origins and reveal a socially circumscribed attitude to nature. The *I Ching* evolved in a society where the social order was fixed but natural phenomena were often untamed: without technology to intervene between man and nature their relationship was intimate and demanded a more sensitive attention than we are accustomed to. The opposite situation characterizes contemporary Western life. These major differences mean that we must inevitably reinterpret the original metaphors of nature in terms which can enlighten the here and now, terms which are essentially psychic as well as social.

The crucial interpretive act involves, as we have seen, identifying each of the eight trigrams with a particular character type which is also associated with one of the eight apexes of the cube. These character types, like the good old man and his partner the bad old woman, have existed from time immemorial as embodiments of fundamental human tendencies defined by the three dimensions of age, gender and morality. As such they are idealized types rather than particular individuals. Yet in everyday life we encounter individuals who approximate the types and within each one of us, these types can be seen as imaging subpersonalities that are more or less active or latent within our psyches. Thus the interplay, particularly the oppositions, between the various types can be seen in both external social context and/or in inner psychic context. I use the word "psychological" to suggest the simultaneous presence of both possibilities, as we move on to demonstrate more in detail how the *I Ching* combines with the cube to clarify ourselves and our time.

Once psychosocial significance has been located in the trigrams, one can see the hexagrams as relations between two trigrams and hence between the people/characters they represent. The basis of the interrelationship, like the basis for moving from one tri- or hexagram to another, is a function of the intensity and direction of the energy involved.

For example, in the hexagram:

the forces for integration are above those for disintegration. The top trigram is forceful and outward going; the lower one moves downward and in. The two avoid each other; in Perls' terms we would have a sterile void; in *I Ching*'s terms we have "standstill"; in psychosocial terms we have the avoidance that exists between the good young man and the evil old woman, the hero and the witch. Heroes have in fact been known to demonstrate their heroism by killing witches.

On the other hand in the hexagram:

䷊

the forces for integration are beneath those for disintegration. The movement of the two trigrams is complementary and they could be said to embrace each other. In terms of the *I Ching* we have "peace" and in terms of psychosocial relationships we have mutual recognition and empathy as opposite energies move into each other.

There are particular rules which govern the steps and hence the paths by which any particular hexagram may transform into any other, but these need not be investigated in detail. The key point is that virtually every throw of the *I Ching* yields a hexagram containing moving lines, that is, strongly broken or strongly unbroken lines. As these transform into their opposites in accordance with the rules, a second-stage hexagram emerges to our contemplation, or in terms of the moving cube, a second character type calls attention to itself. In the case where the character types or the hexagrams are polar opposites, great energy, represented by many intermediate changes, will be necessary.[19] Whatever the distance involved, any apex can relate to any other; there are no relationships which cannot occur. The situation of polar opposites such as we had between "peace" and "standstill" is the most difficult but even there a variety of intermediary hexagrams can be imaged.

Because there is no end, no single center or vantage point, no single goal, state or condition to be attained but only movement, all poles can be brought into awareness and relationship. There is no threat of being stuck since even "standstill" conatins within it usually at least one moving line and always a nuclear hexagram which contains the seeds of change. Since there is no end, there are no catastrophe scripts and the divisions into good and bad which are essential to life can be kept in perspective as mutually necessary. There are no cosmic blanks but only invitations to new life; there is no chaos without seeds of new life. We can have the polarized structures our minds need without fearing or impeding the flow of life. In spite of the mathematical regularity of the hexagrams, the *I Ching* is divided into two unequal halves—the first part of the book has 30 sections whereas the second has 34—because perfect symmetry applied to life would result in stagnation: there must always be a creative imbalance.

The mathematical perfection of the *I Ching* has invited researchers to do statistical studies of the probability of throwing different hexagrams. They have found that the probability of throwing certain hexagrams is higher than that of throwing others.[20] thus moving from one which is easier to obtain to one which is harder takes more energy rather like going uphill. Probabilities however only function in a world where situations are considered repeatable and the assumption of the *I Ching* is that each throw, each moment, is a unique intersection between a person and the stream of life. Thus there is a coexistence of two worlds, in terms of concepts of time, between the linear time of the statistcian which the *I Ching*'s mathematical perfection invites and the synchronic time on which the *I Ching* functions. The inclusiveness of synchronous time which catalyzes the relationships between co-existive phenomena is central to the *I Ching*'s contribution to Western conceptions which have been largely biased by linear time. Open-ended and unending movement keeps our poles of definition interacting so that they can yield significance.

The *I Ching* itself has a comment to make on this process which conveniently culminates the conceptual movement of this whole study so far. It refers to the hexagram *K'un*, the "receptive" in which all lines are broken, hence the hexagram which most concentrates the process of disintegration, hence the maximum openness to the forces of integration. In its ideogram we have the receptive both as underlying stability of the earth and as the motion of the earth's rotation.

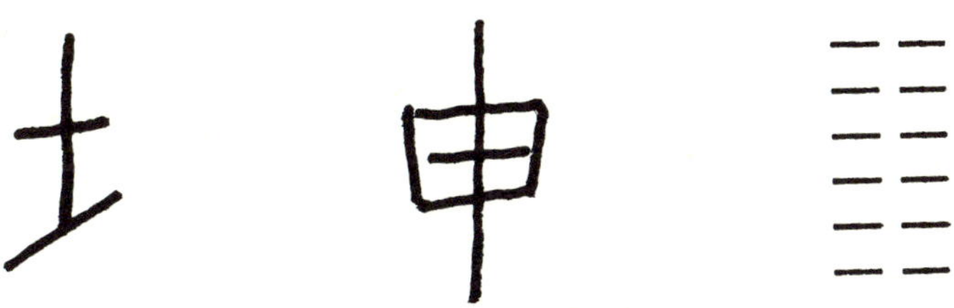

earth's structure earth's rotation

> The symbol of heaven is the circle, and that of earth is the square. Thus squareness is a primary quality of the earth. On the other hand, movement in a straight line, as well as magnitude, is a primary quality of the Creative. But all square things have their origin in a straight line and between lines, planes, and solids, we find that rectangular planes result from straight lines, and cubic magnitudes from rectangular planes. The receptive accommodates itself to the qualities of the creative and makes them its own. Thus a square develops out of a straight line and a cube out of a square. This is compliance with the laws of the creative; nothing is taken away, nothing added. Therefore the receptive has no need of special purposes of its own nor of any effort; yet everything turns out as it should?[21]

This commentary recapitulates in terms of the *I Ching* the movement we have followed through increasingly complex conceptions of the human psyche, each one generating the next most complex structure of ideas as if they were mathematical concepts. Weininger's over-simplifications gave way to Freud's richer but still limited notions, which in turn were superseded by Jung's more balanced concepts, which in turn yielded the fully three-dimensional cube. The cube itself is enriched by the dynamic fourth dimension suggested by Perls' concepts and finds an embodiment in the *I Ching*. In the words of the commentary, "a square develops out of a straight line and a cube out of a square." My analysis so far has simply extended the process, thanks to the *I Ching*, into the fourth dimension which can allow our conceptions to be applicable to human lives through time. In the words of the commentary once more, "this is compliance with the laws of the Creative; nothing is taken away, nothing added."

In Part Two I want to show what specific insights can emerge on the basis of the conceptual work carried out so far. I believe that the cube, set in motion in accordance with the *I Ching*, can yield significant insights into ourselves and our world. In particular these concern women, for whom newly creative images are emerging. As an example of how dynamic cubal concepts can clarify what is happening at this time I refer to my life as it has been moved by the culture changing around me as well as by my changing cultures.

Notes to Chapter 7

1. The *I Ching* has traditionally been consulted by a variety of people in a variety of ways. It has been considered a sacred text and nonsense depending on the period. It has been consulted by priests, emperors and gamblers and was at one time regularly used by the latter to settle debts. Most crudely it has been considered a device for predicting the future; however, if one has read the texts, the difficulties are obvious. The book uses images which do not lead themselves to prediction of specific events. Since every moment has in it an imprint from the past and implications for the future, a profound enough sense of the present is all that is needed.

   The earliest means of consulting the orable was to crack a large bone either in a fire or by striking it with another bone. A master would then read the cracks. The yarrow stick technique involves a practice of meditation: 50 sticks are divided repeatedly in a process which takes about an hour. The most common modern method is the coin method. By throwing three coins 6 times and assigning the yang value of 3 to heads and the yin value of 2 to tails, one builds up a hexagram. See the Wilhelm edition of the *I Ching* for a full explanation. A second coin method exists for those who wish to approximate the probability of the yarrow stick method. Two coins of different sizes are thrown twice for each line, and depending on the sequence and the side that falls up, one arrives at various patterns of 4 which correspond to the lines 6, 7, 8 or 9. See the following chart:

HH	TH	HT	TT	1st letter = smaller coin
9	7	7	7	
HH	HH	HH	TT	2nd letter = larger coin
HH	TH	HT	TT	H = heads = yang
7	9	8	8	
TH	TH	TH	TH	T = tails = yin
HH	TH	HT	TT	2 tosses = 1 throw
7	8	9	8	
HT	HT	HT	HT	1 throw = 1 line
HH	TH	HT	TT	6 lines = 1 hexagram
8	8	8	6	
TT	TT	TT	TT	

A third method involves the use of cubal dice. This method retains the probability of the yarrow stalk method and introduces an increased invitation to projection. Instead of building up a hexagram step by step, all the elements are given at once, thus the thrower is prevented from the inevitable attempts to guess what the next line will be. A temporal process is replaced by a sudden configuration and a potential intellectual analysis by a potential intuitive insight.

2. Chinese Acupuncturist and student of the *I Ching*, Jing N. Wu, gave a lecture on Jan. 9, 1979, at Les Cedres, Chene-Bourg, Geneva, Switzerland in which he talked about the meaning of certain ideograms and the origins of various practices. He also received me personally on Jan. 12 at the home of the Whites, Veyrier, Geneva, Switzerland.
3. *I Ching*, pp. 280-1.
4. Wu, Jan. 9.
5. The strong yin line is 6 and changes into a yang line: 7. ⟶ ⟵ becomes ——— .
The strong yang line is 9 and changes into a yin line: 8. ⟵⟶ becomes — — .
The unchanging yin line is 8 and the unchanging yang line, 7. Changing strong lines into their yin/yang opposites thereby generates a second hexagram which plots out probable evolutions from the state of the first hexagram.

   Even if a hexagram is made up of all 7 and 8, hence unchanging lines, it nonetheless has in it a nuclear hexagram which can indicate evolution. It is composed of the inner 4 lines of a hexagram rearranged as follows:

6 — —	5 — —
5 — —	4 ———
4 ———	3 ———
3 ———	4 ———
2 — —	3 ———
1 — —	2 — —

6. Lao Tzu, *Tao Teh Ching: The Way and Its Power*, trans. Arthur Waley (London: Allen & Unwin, 1934), p. 155.
7. Daniel Goleman, "Holographic Memory," *Psychology Today*, 12, No. 9 (Feb. 1979), p. 79.

8. Goleman, p. 84.
9. Goleman, p. 83.
10. Goleman, p. 80
11. Former student of C, G. Jung and Jungian analyst and writer, Marie-Louise von Franz, lectured on August 9, 1978 at Eranos in the Tessin, Switzerland on concepts of time.
12. *I Ching*, p. xxix.
13. *I Ching*, p. xxviii.
14. *I Ching*, p. xxviii.
15. Wu, Jan. 9.
16. *I Ching*, pp. 262-3.
17. In any case, adaptation and reinterpretation of the Oriental original are inescapable if we are to profit from the insights of the original. Joe Havens has recently demonstrated this point in relation to yoga by extending traditional notions in *A Fifth Yoga: The Way of Relationships* to include encounter and empathy with the otherness of other persons as central to a Western yoga. It underlines the Western need for attending to the social relationships that are in the process of change.
18. See footnote 5 above.
19. To move from one hexagram to the other, all of the lines would have to be six or nine, i.e. changing lines. Needless to say this represents considerable investment of energy. Since the lines could change in any order, the path between the two could take several directions or in other words there are many internediate hexagram which might represent stages along the way. One trajectory might be:

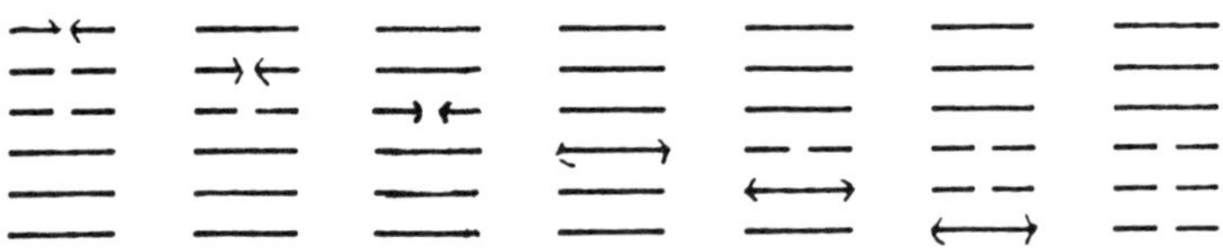

20. Ken Phillips, computer specialist and student of the *I Ching* lectured at the Jung Institute in Zurich, Switzerland in June 1978. He created a periodic table of the 64 hexagrams which corresponds to the chemical periodic table presenting one with the relative difficulty any given hexagram encounters in the process of changing to any other. The difficulty is a result of the difference in probability with which given hexagrams occur.
21. *I Ching*, p. 13.

Part II

There is at bottom only one problem in the world, this is its name. How does one break through? How does one get into the open? How does one burst the cocoon and become a butterfly?

Thomas Mann

I
Culture Change

In order to show how dynamic cubal concepts can clarify contemporary experience the following pages treat psychological perspectives in two separate phases, first the social, then the individual. In both cases the focus is on cross-cultural experience, not simply because it is central to my life and to the mating of Western and Eastern modes of conceptualization, but still more because moments of intense cross-cultural experience give a condensed and highlighted capsule of what happens in everyday life. At moments of dramatic change, particularly moving into an unfamiliar culture, we can have a clearer insight into the dynamics of self-identification in terms of the character types already associated with the cube and the *I Ching*.

It thus makes sense to begin with the experience of changing cultures because this social perspective focuses on the external factors that are imposed on every individual who moves from a familiar to a foreign culture. This focus is all the more relevant to the present study because, as we shall see, whenever families are involved such moves are particularly difficult for women and hence their psychosocial experience particularly invites attentive analysis. In addition even those who remain stable must adapt to the changes going on around them either because neighbors have moved or because the culture in general is changing faster now than ever before.

Let us begin by imagining an individual who has established a reasonably stable self, or in cubal terms, has established a fruitful complementarity among the various character-type tendencies that inhabit the different apexes of the person's cube. Moving from residency in one culture to another obviously upsets the status quo. The die, the cube, whatever configuration of self-identification one has been living on, is cast. Once set in motion, it can never return to its earlier state because the relations between the various apexes are modified irreversibly. As

Thomas Wolfe put it, "You Can't Go Home Again"—because *you* have changed and if for no other reason, so has your home culture as you perceive it. Like initiation, culture change changes one's outlook; one can no longer believe in the "naturalness" of any cultural concept, not even the idea of "nature" itself. A person who changes cultures is soon disabused of what Ernest Becker in *The Denial of Death* describes as the "cultural lie" which by claiming for itself ultimate powers of life and death functions to screen out from everyday consciousness our awareness of human nature and human mortality.

> *We have seen that what we call human character is actually a lie about the nature of reality...a pretense that one is invulnerable because protected by the power of others and of culture, that one is important in nature and can do something about the world.*[1]

Of course, sooner or later most human individuals come to this realization, but shared cultural presumptions tend to discourage awareness of the arbitrariness central to all cultures. Thus Parisians (and others!) think it "natural" to prune trees in certain shapes, as if otherwise they might die. Even "nothing" can become something:

Dialogue: foreign mother and local teacher on the day before school:

"What should my child bring to school?"

"Oh, nothing. We provide everything."

Same teacher and mother the first day after school:

"Where are your child's bedroom slippers?"

"I thought you said she needed nothing."

"Oh, but of course....everyone knows...."

As a resident of a strange land one constantly rubs against the shared local presumptions so well established as to have been forgotten. One begins to feel like a rift in the world of the established others, and they on the other hand like a rift in your world.

Initiation rites served to mediate between different domains in moments of transition. Traditionally these were prescribed at certain ages and marked into a different but fixed relationship to society. The sacred moment was the one which lay between the old role and the moment of change when one is especially vulnerable. Similarly rites of hospitality governed interactions with strangers who if not in transition were in transit and similarly vulnerable. They, like the initiate in the liminal stage, were outside of a known social context.

The charged character of the stranger has been reflected in rituals and in religious texts:

> *"Be not forgetful of strangers and travellers."*[2]
> *"Hospitality to stangers is greater than reverence for the name of God."*[3]
> *"I was a stranger and you took me in."*[4]

Among the Bedouins the greeting to a stranger is, "You are among your family,"[5] and it is backed up by the offer of a bath, a meal and shelter for three days. Similar customs have been found among Greeks, Danish, British, Romans, Japanese. In ancient Israel and Greece introductory questions or exchange of information was forbidden until after the guest has enjoyed the hospitality of bath and food. Such restrictions, like the nature of the gifts offered, make explicit the significance of the ritual. The bond was based on a common humanity, symbolized verbally in several languages (Greek—xenos, Latin—hospes, French—hote, Italian—ospite) by one word meaning both host and guest. The ambivalence of the stranger is also represented by the language where hospitality and hostility share a common root. The need for food, water and shelter transcend all social categories. Thus, the offer of hospitality had to precede these exchanges of information which would compromise the quality of stranger with fixed categories of friend or foe, rich or poor.

The stranger then is half known, half unknown; half human, half other; half "cultural," half "natural." As such he, for traditionally women stayed at home, shares the characteristics of many hybrid deities. A hybrid constitution often assures the "otherness," the specialness of a deity. Jesus was both human and divine; Pan was both human and animal, for example. Otherness is incomprehensible if not part familiar. This otherness was originally sacred in the sense of taboo—a source of power or energy before being differentiated into good and bad, into good Jesus and bad Pan, good divine and bad animal. The stranger however has retained an original ambivalence.

Although today the media saturate us with cultural stereotypes of other nationalities, the actual experience of being a stranger retains much of its ambivalence. The fantastic success of such phenomena as *Star Trek*, *Star Wars* and *Close Encounters of The Third Kind* is perhaps a response to a basic need for an alien around which to project alien parts of ourselves. Whereas in early science fiction the alien was a dangerous threat, recently, especially since *Star Trek*, the alien has emerged as a positive figure. In *Star Trek* Spock, half Vulcan, half human, is a crucial part of the crew of the Enterprise without whom many conflicts could not be resolved; nonetheless he retains a certain dangerous aspect through his special powers.

This dual aspect of the stranger seems to constellate what is familiar as well as foreign; in short, polar opposites seem to be called into play. In the world of Islam, Allah, who is usually rather remote, comes to earth as an unknown trickster, "The Green One"; Elias of the Old Testament comes to earth as the "unknown visitor" often appearing as one of a rejected group—a beggar, an Arab, a Negro or a prostitute for example.[6] In contemporary terms Spock, for example, is described in terms of his most human and ordinary of mothers as well as in terms of his alien Vulcan powers. In terms of the cube he could be seen as a combination of the good mother and the trickster. Spock's mother is named Amanda, deriving from the Latin verb to love; Spock's Vulcan physiology is full of tricks—his heart is where his liver should be, his blood is green, etc.

In terms of actually being an alien in a foreign land similar polarities are triggered. In addition to being the rift in the everyday world, the stranger is also the epitome of that world through being perceived as a cultural stereotype. In this way the stranger has that liminal status Sherry Ortner described as characteristic of women who, on the margins of society are symbols of either transcendence or subversion.[7] The stranger and the woman are more or less than others but never peers. Similarly just as one feels either pleasure or displeasure at the unexpected, so the stranger is rarely "neutral." The stranger always seems to elicit a charged response.

In the absence of hospitality rituals in modern society the problem for the stranger is first of all to recognize and identify the various characteristics of his/her state, the first of which is vulnerability. Then the problem is how to cope with them, with this in-between world, this gap which opens when one becomes aware of oppositions. Similar kinds of discontinuities appear in other circumstances. For example, aging can bring on discontinuities in one's perception of oneself: others can act toward you as if you were older than you feel inside or vice versa. However this is a gradual change, whereas cultural change is abrupt. Overnight one must cope with the crack that opens between two worlds.

> *Twilight may be the crack between the ordinary and nonordinary worlds because it is a time of uncertain perception, when imagination plays a greater part in what we see.*[8]

This area used to be that sacred space created by ritual observances; it is still protected by the psychiatrist's office, or the space created by therapy or encounter groups. However, the stranger is typically unprepared and unprotected.

To borrow the terms of ritual, the place one is leaving to enter the liminal stage is the self-image and/or the stereotype; the place one is going toward is one's as yet unknowable other self. Because of their unknown dimension the strangers around you invite projection, just as you do for them. Thus the first problem is understanding the polarity set up both between your self-image and your other self and between you as stereotype to others and you as ambiguous alien.The certainty of the former can be counter part to the anxiety associated with ambiguous otherness.

Projection produces dependency on that environment on which one is projecting one's own inner energy. Whereas Perls encouraged the individual to reclaim these forces by playing their parts and incorporating them into oneself, such a person is rarely the first one you meet in a foreign country. On the contrary the function of most societies is to assure your fidelity to prescribed roles—hardly an invitation to integrating foreign parts of oneself.

In addition to dependency, feelings of anxiety and anger arise. Anxiety is the natural reaction to a situation where one does not know what role to play. Hostility easily results from the many misunderstandings which result from different expectations about appropriate behavior in different circumstances. Above all hostility is the inescapable response to others who seem to exploit the foreigner's situation of dependence. An obvious example is being overcharged and not having the right vocabulary handy to defend yourself.

As a projection screen everyone becomes potentially a liminal figure, a shape-shifter who tricks you in any variety of ways. Moral categories are redefined: lying can be considered a necessary survival skill in a traditional bureaucratic society. Physical categories also change: nudity in a doctor's office, for example, can be quite acceptable in Europe and not in the States. Psychological categories are made ambiguous by one's own and others' projections. The extraordinary degree to which humans can see what they want is brought out in a study interviewing men who went to prostitutes. Virtually all of the prostitutes frequented were considered young and beautiful, qualities which the interviewer found on verification to be quite absent. Few of the men, moreover, could describe with any precision the characteristics of the woman they frequented.[9] A largely anonymous situation similar to that which exists between prostitute and client often applies when someone encounters a stranger, who is inevitably perceived as transient.

In addition then to the dependency, anxiety and hostility the stranger can count on, one can trigger a variety of unexpected responses by appearing to others to be a shape-shifter. One is supposed to fulfill the expected stereotype of one's nation (or race or class or sex) and above all one becomes threatening when one does with ease actions forbidden to natives. It is not possible for a single woman to walk alone in certain parts of North Africa without being treated like a prostitute. Furthermore any indignation she might register will only aggravate the natives' indigation.

Since there are analogies between the condition of culture change and the liminal states within all human beings, let's see if the latter can give us clues to the form crises will take and if we can use the cube to clarify what might otherwise appear as disorder.

First of all same-side oppositions are called forth on the face of the cube which corresponds to the gender of the person undergoing change. Jung spoke of the wise old man having a negative aspect. This pairing is dramatized in *The Teachings of Don Juan*[10] by Castenada. For example Don Juan is described as having short white hair and deep wrinkles with eyes having a light of their own. Mescalito, however, had eyes that were gold and black, a head that was pointed like a strawberry, and skin that is green and warty. The former description recalls very much the warm good old man as friendly guide just as the latter reflects a dwarfish vegetation numen. The wise old man functions hand in hand with the trickster.

The trickster calls forth the projective raw material of dreams and imagery; the wise old man calls forth interpretative wisdom which gives the trickster's chaotic richness comprehensible form. Metaphor, symbol and finally myth can potentially emerge from such a union of conscious and unconscious. The individual needs to be aware that each needs the other.

Castenada, the anthropologist, made such complementary sense of both sides. He went so far as to kneel before the plants the trickster told him to even if he could not actually talk to them. He also accepted the teachings of Don Juan who in the end affirms all views of reality as just that—views. He converted through his writing this experience of threshold living into creative output. He had the "coordinates" of his training into which he could read out his experiences from this other world. He entered this realm knowing he had the coordinates, the training, and consciously choosing his path. He exhibited all the attributes of the good, young man; he was pursuing his own goals with the energy of integration.

Thus women entering culture change are in a very different situation from that of men since there are few cultural precedents for change for women. First of all there is no religious tradition through which to find analogies with a state of transformation. Men's rites of passage initiate them into culture through dramatically separating them from nature and the mother who embodies the forces of nature. Women when they do have such rites of passage from one stage in their lives to another, for example at the onset of menstruation, find themselves affirming their identity with nature![11] Whereas boys' initiation rites include revelation of a sacred object and an origin myth, girls' rites include only the secret meaning of a natural phenomenon. Whereas boys are initiated in a group to culture, girls are initiated alone back into nature. For example, menstruation rites must be solitary if they are to correspond to the natural variation of individual menstruation. By remaining secure within the identity of their bodies, they do not undergo the experiences which are intended to change their psychological perspectives in such a way as to be more aware of an inner self distinct from nature or social role and capable of undergoing change, and eventually of choosing how one wants to change. In a similar perspective hospitality rites never applied to women as strangers since they never travelled. On the other hand, a wife might be offered to a stranger as part of his accommodations.

In so far as women have been kept dependent on men they do not have a sense of individual will; in so far as their identity has depended on traditionally stable roles made by and for men, they have few mental images or role models for alternative ways of life. The mothering role has been a woman's main source of identity, from before Weininger through Jung and indeed beyond him. Although Perls' degenderized vocabulary is very liberating, it cannot provide specific transsexual models because of its extreme openness.

Women entering culture change are in a bind. First of all they are usually accompanying their families, a fact alone which underlines their dependent condition. The state of being in a new cultural context further emphasizes this. Also they probably have had insufficient access to language courses and other basic training appropriate to the combat at hand. On the other hand super competence is demanded of them by the expectations of their families. Especially if there are children, the mothers must recreate "home," that oasis of familiarity to which everyone else can return having been battered by the new world's battles. Not only are they asked to recreate a home environment that is perhaps more "typical" than it would have been in their native land, but in addition they are seen in the eyes of the natives as stereotypes of their particular nationality. Thus, on the one hand, they are "stuck" or in the terms of the *I Ching* they are "squares," stereotypical representatives of the "feminine." Being a square is slang for being stuck, i.e. a representative of a moribund social order. On the other hand they are poorly trained to cope with many new experiences of their own.

These new experiences often lead to identity confusion. Not knowing how to do simple things makes one appear and feel stupid just when one is expected to be most competent. Not knowing how one is to be taken provides anxiety. Being taken as someone one did not want to project can create hostility and anger. Seeing others act in ways one cannot permit oneself also provokes anger. Roles are unconsciously known from one's own culture; even in the States where the rate of change is probably higher than anywhere else in the world, most people still have some handle on what is expected. In Europe roles are more tightly defined, less subject to inquiry and less publicly analyzed. Whether a woman likes it or not she has to move into her "bad" areas: she may appear to be an incompetent mother by handling her children differently, a promiscuous wife by appearing alone in public, a shrew or bitch by getting angry or defending herself.

First of all, anger and hostility are some of the most difficult feelings for women to cope with. In cubal terms only the witch/bitch gets angry. Anger then excites guilt which threatens one's increased dependency status. There are places where simply being a woman alone implies one is sexually available. All of a sudden one finds oneself coping with one's "bad" side both in terms of how one appears to others and vice versa. Few women these days enjoy being taken as sex objects especially when the guilt implicit there becomes a manipulative tool.

Whether or not one knows the language becomes very important. Studies indicate that a person who is abruptly placed among speakers of another language can develop paranoid tendencies[12] which might be more or less justified depending on the degree of hostility projected onto the foreigner. Once again psychological factors are called into play in the act of learning a language. Learning it on the spot makes one like a child in relation to the native speaker, a situation which may feel threatening even to someone with a strong sense of self. Then a point is reached at which one can easily or adequately "get along"[13]: one's speech is understood and vice versa, though mistakes continue. At this point the "learner" has to voluntarily accept the dependency role she has just outgrown and invite the native speaker to offer those corrections which while inessential would improve his/her language ability and the acceptance that implies. Accepting the dependency also implies accepting the tendency to anger which is still there whenever one feels exploited; it also implies accepting the validity of another culture, even once one recognizes the arbitrariness that characterizes every culture.

The Thursday Thing

Every Thursday for three months a group of approximately twenty women met around the theme of culture change. We called our gathering The Thursday Thing, going back to the roots of "thing" which derives from the Icelandic word meaning assembly of people and that's what we were. Ages ranged from 27 to 55, length of time in Geneva from three months to eighteen years, civil status included everything but the widow. Ten nationalities were represented including one Swiss from the German-speaking part of the country. All had direct cross-cultural experience to digest.

The most general feeling shared by those present was that of being stuck in a rut. Some blamed this on Geneva despite its large foreign population and its history as a "native" place for multicultural people. Many of these women felt frustrated in their personal, especially professional, goals since work permits are often excluded for dependents; many felt a lack of profundity in their lives. Perhaps this superficiality derives from transience and from the kind of escapism it can inculcate. One woman who moved every two or three years said she felt that she had never come to terms with life in the same way as others who led more settled lives. Such people choose to be aliens. Perhaps once one has made the first move and felt the gap between the cultural lie and oneself, it is easier to become a professional alien than to explore the gap which is created. Repetition of the experience of moving may replace exploration of the tension endemic to the act itself.

Women experiencing culture change must face the discrepancy between themselves and their roles abruptly; nonetheless this is the same problem women all over the world are confronting in different ways. In this sense the group of women I worked with here in Geneva seemed like a microcosm for the tensions behind the women's movement. The inherited culturally defined crusts of consciousness are not satisfying women's needs to fulfill a call to fuller human stature. The tendency of the women's movement to destroy old roles as inadequate shells can threaten the new life that needs protection and does not deal with the problem of creating new roles which correspond to the new life emerging on the inside. Nonetheless it is perhaps the necessary reaction to having denied the person for the role so long. This is the opposite situation to that of the professional alien who sacrifices her inner self to the repeated act of recreating "home" again and again. She is safer from change by staying on the road than she would be in the States. The creative gap is rather like an energy field that stretches between the conscious and unconscious, between the role or fact of roles and the inner person.

Being stuck is being repetitive and interestingly enough many women in the group got unstuck when they did something new, something they had never done before, and realized it. A couple of them went to school; one who had been trying to recreate a career left behind in New York went to New York only to learn that it was not at all as she remembered it. She realized she had chosen to feel alienated rather than try to find something she could do here. One woman when she realized that she had had her children here, also realized that she could never know what it would have been like to have been a mother in London. Although her children speak French as their native language and call Geneva home, she still calls home where her parents are and imagines returning there to die, all the while knowing with part of herself that her "home" is in her head. One evening we had access to video equipment and watched ourselves recreate the subgroup identities in terms of which we felt alienated. Although we all spoke fluent English, the Italians addressed other Italians, British conversed with British, Americans Americans, etc. We recreated the national and social distinctions we felt had been imposed upon us by an external social situation which included wives' dependency on husbands as well as the status of foreigner.

Although we did many things together—discussed short stories which themselves turned on crises, shared experience—one of the most interesting evenings was a joint meeting with a "native" women's group. Here we discovered that out of thirty-five participants only one was Genevese; nonetheless half felt native while half felt alien. We were obliged to see how personal choice was involved, although fluency in French and access to jobs were unanimously characteristic of the group of "natives" and only partially characteristic of the "aliens."

In spite of the variety of topics discussed, stories read and activities undertaken, there was no special technique; nonetheless after thirteen meetings few would say they still felt alienated. Simple awareness of the feelings involved and of the presence of others who share them provided all that was needed in many cases. That awareness and sharing itself was a new undertaking, a break with repetition.

Culture change, then, provokes a crisis by on the one hand exaggerating the familiar as we saw in playing the stereotype or recreating the old "home" and on the other hand by provoking shape-shifting and encounters with the unknown. The former stimulates conscious acquisitions, the latter unconscious projections, hence the field between the poles is energized. The element of choice seems to enter when one is aware of both poles and can refuse one of them either by denying oneself or the culture or by accepting them and trying to bring them into a creative and complementary relationship. Lack of access to language and work compromises one's possibilities for creatively using the tension. Out of the women's group only two, a writer and an artist, found the lack of access to public life a positive force for their work and development. Nonetheless the tension can be eased in many ways.

Crisis comes from the Greek meaning "decision, judgment, event, issue, turning point of a disease" (OED). The "energy field" between the conscious world of stuckness and the unconscious one of projections is activated and tension is produced in so far as one keeps these two worlds separate. A state of tension demands resolution or release, something has to be done. Releasing the tension involves bringing the elements of the conflict into complementary relationship. Given the social pressure to keep good and bad discrete especially in relation to women, women are often placed in a more difficult position than men by this situation. Attempts to relate to their projected and often rejected selves can involve them in a moral conflict. In order to claim all of themselves they often have to accept social criticism if not rejection. One of the functions of a group is to create a "subsociety" where one can find support.

One woman in the Thursday Thing moved though this process with us unusually clearly and beautifully. When she arrived, she was feeling or was showing the feeling most dramatically of being stuck and in a crisis. She was very anxious and began to express her worries over simply being away from home for one evening. Although she was through raising her children, her husband saw her as mother and became agitated when she was away. Other women shared some supporting experiences about their husbands or others, always ending on the note that even if daddy had a fit when mommy went to visit her daughter in Switzerland or whatever, she did it nonetheless. We all wanted her to continue to come and she did, gradually seeming more at ease. One evening she shared with us her fantasy: she wanted to run a hotel where she could use all the qualities of competence she had to hide from her husband with whom she had to appear dependent and helpless. She at first felt it was an unrealizable dream. Everyone in the group was immediately energized and fleshed out her fantasy: it would be a hotel for women decorated by one of the group members who was an artist. We told her how she could reinterpret her years as a maid and mother (she quit school to be a private maid at 14 and married at 17) and present them as administrative experience. She left feeling very good. We heard no more about the hotel but at the evaluation session she began the evening by saying how comfortable she felt with herself. She said she thought that starting a hotel at 47 was not worth the trouble. She was reconciled to her present position. I know little about it but I can see that it has been modified enough that she can at least leave one night a week alone not only without anxiety but with pleasure.

In terms of the cube I would see her as one in whom mother and daddy's little girl were united: her life though one of caring for others was first of all one of duty to a male authority. Her appearance of incompetence was necessary to enhance his feeling of power and authority; her need was to realize her own masculinity, in terms of both recognized competence and authority. Her world is relatively uncomplex, as she is the first to admit, and the division between masculine and feminine seems sharp and simple and perhaps still too undifferentiated to fit fully with the cube.Nonetheless her story demonstrates how stuckness and tension were resolved by a decision to do something—coming to the group, and a willingness to look at one's other side—sharing her fantasy of having power, competence and authority. Whatever she decides to do at a later date the group response made her feel that these characteristics were rightfully hers. Perhaps she will not do anything as complicated as starting a hotel but she may undertake some enterprise that will use her skills and experience.

Her "crisis" kept her turning round the conflict between the public fact of having to act out a role of dependency and incompetence and the inner fact of independence and competence. Making a decision to look at and accept both parts of herself, the good and the bad, already provided relief. Enabled by a supportive network to contemplate the images of what her intellect and role condemned, she could bring oppositions into creative complementarity.

The *I Ching* presents an interesting perspective on the possibilities of the different relationships between good and evil.

This hexagram would represent the good old man "understanding" his same gender polar opposite, the bad young man (the trickster). Unlike the hexagram where the hero understands the witch, the movement of the energy is unstable. The two trigrams head toward each other creating the state of tension which seeks release in revolution. Since the center of gravity is central such changes as revolution involves need not be feared.

This hexagram presents the good old man, the one preferred by society standing on top of the bad young man. His energy merges with that of the trickster who, scorned by society (and Jung) is underneath. This is the hexagram of revolution, insight and inner truth.

We can take a comparable situation in relation to women: Cinderella is persecuted by her wicked stepmother and must be saved by Prince Charming. There is no way for her to relate to the stepmother creatively by herself. Once again the hexagrams of the *I Ching* reveal the dynamics of these relationships. When we have Cinderella under the thumb of the wicked stepmother, we have the hexagram "darkening of the light" in which earth conceals but does not distinguish the light. The light must wait just as Cinderella depends on Prince Charming to pull her upward through obstacles like poverty or the wicked stepmother into freedom from their obstructions. Then Cinderella belongs above the wicked stepmother.

Or we can take the situation of the woman in the Thursday Thing. If we see her as mother trying to relate to her inner "son" her young creative masculinity, we could get the following hexagrams:

Here the vigorous son stands above the mother giving the hexagram "retreat'. There is nothing that can be done but withdraw to avoid a life-and-death struggle and wait for better times. The energy of the top trigram moves up and away from the lower one which can only stand still. Aversion leaves one stuck.

Here in "taming power of the great" the mother is above the son and great energy is present. The strong line at the top stores the rising energy of the creative son beneath. Once again the creative relationship is based on complementary direction of energy. The socially acceptable relationship places the mother as subordinate to the son,or the daughter to the stepmother, or the trickster to the wise old man, but in all of these the energy flow between the two trigrams is in opposite directions resulting in some sort of standstill. The complementary relationship between opposing forces releases the creative possibility.

I had originally chosen to use short stories as a focus for the group because they are about crises; however we shifted to our own personal experience since culture change is a unique example of alienation. Similarly rather than try to understand my own crises and the relevance of the cube second-hand through the fictions of others, I want to move now to an analysis of the crises provoked at entry and reentry into new cultures, and of the cube which emerged out of them and helped me through them. If fictions can be called frames for making sense, then the cube is a key fiction which aids reflections on social and personal experience.

Notes to Chapter 1

1. Becker, p. 187.
2. Assembly of Princes, China, 650 B.C.E. as cited in Robert E. Meagher, "Strangers at The Gate," *Parabola*, 2, No. 4, p. 10.

3. Hebrew proverb as cited in Meagher, p. 10.
4. Gospel of Matthew as cited in Meagher, p. 10.
5. Meagher, p. 11
6. Lecture by Marie-Louise von Franz on the Stranger at the Jung Institute in June 1975.
7. Ortner, p. 86.
8. Whan, p. 198.
9. Charles Winich, "Prostitutes' Clients' Perception of the Prostitutes and of Themselves." *The Lively Commerce: Prostitution in The United States.* New York: Quadrangle 1971, pp. 289-297.
10. Carlos Castaneda, *The Teachings of Don Juan: A Yaqui Way of Knowledge* (New York: Ballantine Books, 1969).
11. Eliade, p. 82.
12. F. F. Kino, "Aliens' Paranoid Reactions" in *Uprooting and After...*, ed. Charles Zwingmann and Maria Pfister Ammende (New York: Springer, 1973), pp. 64-5.
13. See Paul LaForge, *Research Profiles with Community Language Learning* (Apple River, Illinois: Counseling-Learning Institutes, 1975), Part I.

2
Personal Crises

Having developed the concept of the cube in relation to psychological models of the twentieth century with the important addition of the *I Ching* to complement Western preconceptions, I want to show its working application. In order to illustrate this I had to choose between the life of a fictional character or characters and the life of someone I knew well, better than anyone in the Thursday Thing, even if one of those women were willing to share more of their personal lives. On reflection I realized that I knew no one better than myself and that so far I have been the only person to have lived with the cube through all its stages of evolution.

Although all lives are in a continual process of change, culture change is to the small daily steps in evolution as an earthquake is to the small daily slippages that go on around a 'fault:' it is a sudden shift in one's sense of reality. Culture change is dramatic and cannot be ignored. It is a kind of macrocosmic indicator of change. Thus my own life tensions have been most sharply crystallized around times of culture change. At these dramatic moments of sudden shift in external circumstances the functioning of the cube becomes most obvious in the attempt to resolve such crises. Since the cube has emerged as I have tried to cope with these experiences, it can now be presented itself as the framework which makes my own experience understandable.

When my personal life seemed too dense and overwhelming to deal with directly, I had wanted to use fiction as a mirror through which to see and better understand it. In addition I wanted to confront directly the fact that critics write their own fiction, a kind of secondary one based on the raw material of the work of art. Recourse to the claim that the meaning lies in the work of art itself or in the author's "real" intentions has seemed like a refusal of responsibility. Meaning cannot exist outside of a context; therefore, in spite of issues of history and sociology, the most weighty context is that created by the reader and his/her needs which change. Recourse to the author poses similar problems. First of all, that person is no longer who s/he was when writing the book in question and in fact can find different meanings in the work as s/he changes. Second, the author's intentions in no way limit what others can see in a given work of fiction. Since the author is no longer the person who wrote the work in question and since the reader/critic creates the most immediate context for interpretation, it seemed most honest to deal directly with the intersection between one's life and the work of fiction.

I explained this position in the Thursday Thing, saying that I wanted to take the short story as an object and use it as a catalyst for exploring our experience. In the first five meetings it worked; however, as we began to feel more comfortable with each other we realized how the specificity of our own experience was left out if we had to keep referring to another's fiction, another's interpretation of another's life history. In addition, the context in which the different members read a given story slanted their interpretation. On the most superficial level the one who read it hurriedly on a bus felt differently about it than the one who read it at leisure in the evening. The only way to share the experience of the story would be to read it aloud together and then discuss it. Since the act of observing changes the data, we needed to share both elements in order to create a common experience.

These complications encouraged me in several ways to use my own experience now rather than fiction. Before our own time, when fiction was the main way of stopping the flow of experience to find meaning in it, the situation was different. But now we all have access to cameras, tape recorders and typewriters with which to create and look at our own fictions. There is no need for an intermediate interpretive screen. And as I became more comfortable with myself, there was no need for the protection of a distracting device. Furthermore, I am the only one to have lived with the cube, which has related to my life experience in very special ways and emerged out of my need for meaning.

Since dipping into one's personal life involves talking of others directly, I had reservations about intruding on people's privacy. However, I once again recalled that observation changed the data, that all interaction including observation is relational. Therefore I will refer to relationships not to individuals. When, for example, I speak of "my mother," I am expressing my perceptions of those relationships that had a particularly charged impact on me. Other people in other situations would see them differently. In addition we are all changing; therefore, persons I met in the past are no longer as they were, and neither am I; the relationship we had may well have changed in the course of time. For me personally, the act of writing is itself a transformative experience. Thus I make no claim to describe anyone, including myself, in any absolute terms: I will use no proper names.

In view of this, I could accurately add: concerning the characters that will emerge in the following pages "Any resemblance to persons living or dead is purely coincidental."

My first impulse was to call this section "chaos," which is what one's personal experience feels like when it is still too dense and overwhelming. However, from the perspective of the cube chaos can be described as the feel of inner space when one has lost one's familiar sense of orientation. Although the common view sees chaos as preceeding an order which emerges out of it, in fact chaos only seems to exist for humans in relation to a preconceived idea of order and how things *ought* to be. Thus it is less chaos than a special relation to the cube. Chaos then is a word for being stuck in a crisis. To understand crisis situations in cubal terms we need to return to the geometry of the cube. There are eight apexes to the cube, each of which has a polar opposite. In fact there are only four polar axes any one of which may become crucial for clarifying or crystallizing any given circumstance, as we shall see. Together any two opposites establish between them a central axis around which the cube can be seen as spinning like a top. A spinning cube becomes conceptually equivalent to a sphere which does not offer any fixed points of reference except for the poles around which one continues to move dizzyingly. The following diagrams show how a spinning cube creates a visually curved form.

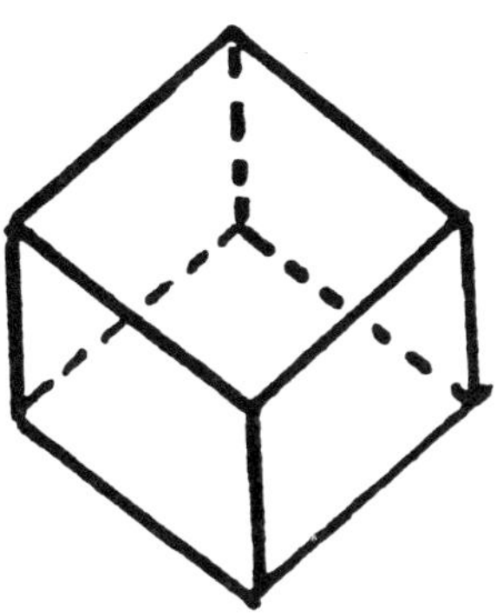

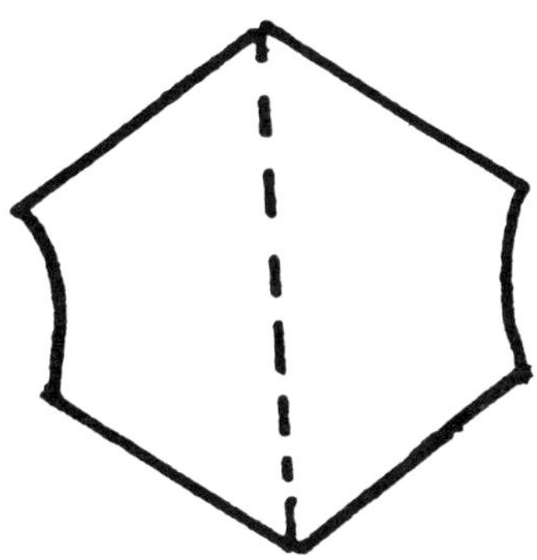

These crises make demands on a person similar to those of changing cultures: one remains stuck until the conflicting forces are brought into a complementary relationship. In fact for me each major culture change provoked a crisis that needed cubal resolution. Since these poles are the reiterated points, they fixate one's attention until the crisis is resolved, until a decision is made. The possible decisions are at bottom few. In a crisis one is in much the same position as the infant who can decide to accept nourishment and live or refuse it and die. We can agree to relate positively to both of the polar axes which are virtually forcing themselves on us and in fact have something to offer us in conjunction with each other. Or we can refuse their nourishment and remain stuck, spinning around and around on the same axis.

My decision to get inside the cube was itself a "crucial"one. Originally I had been trying to use it as a tool external to myself by which to reveal imbalances in society or literature or popular culture such as I had through analysing "Star Trek" episodes. I wanted it as a measure to justify the anger I felt as a woman at having a more limited social slot than that available to men. But at a difficult moment I felt raw and flayed with nowhere to go, no one to turn to. I felt I was at an impasse or sick point Perls described. I felt like a sick helpless child with all its support systems gone. I got into my cube; I made it an incubator.

On December 5, 1978, I wrote in my journal: "My cube landed today and here I am in it. I must get to know it from the inside. It is mine, my prison, my incubator and potentiality, my prism. I must first put my child in the cube as in an incubator; and then I must meditate in the cube and find my center. I have looked over the dreams from the past—there is a wound there that never heals. Maybe I can find its closure in the cube."

Every day I mentally visited the child in the cube watching it grow, turn over, sit up, smile. Every day I meditated in the cube placing the good side behind me for support, the young side under me with their energy rising up through me, the old above me with their greater experience and concern protecting me, the women on my right, the side of the mind, and the men on my left, the side of the heart. For the first time I could confront my earliest memory, that of an enraged father figure. Whereas habitually through earlier years his rage had combined with my need for a supportive father to produce an overwhelming situation, the cube now provided a safer and more realistic framework of many relationships.

From this perspective I could use the four polar relationships built into the cube to understand the major crises of my life. Each of them occurred at a point of entry or reentry into a culture; the resolution of each of them involved first of all an understanding of the situation through words or images and then some action which confirmed the understanding. The first crisis, that constellated by the polar opposition between the good young girl and the evil old man, between myself as infant and my angry father, was at the bottom of the wound that never healed and interfered with the closure of two other crisis points: that polarized between the evil young man and the good mother and that between the good old man and the evil young woman. The first called up my fear of male anger, the second my need for a supportive father, both of which were still such overwhelming feelings that they prevented positive approaches to the male figures involved. The necessary breakthrough came when I could myself embody the forces of the good young man in relation to the bad old woman: out of this crisis emerged the urge to incubate the original crisis between the good young girl and the bad old man.

In the following pages I will deal with each of the four crises first in terms of the situation within which they occurred then in terms of the cubal images and related actions through which they became understandable and resolvable.

Entry into the United States

My entry into the United Sates occurred with my birth, about which I remember nothing. When I think about describing the context into which I was born, I am amazed at how little I know of the parents who had me. Almost everything has to be pieced together from what I have been told later by others.

My "father" was accustomed until the Depression to all the amenities servants guarantee. He had finished law school and was working when he and my mother met. He was charmed by my mother's naiveté and apparent innocence.She came from a farming community. The first in her family to get a college education, she graduated before her time, a woman who risked leaving home and competing in a man's world. My mother found a job with the same company my father worked for. There they met and soon married. My mother probably acted the perfect "daddy's little girl," whose unworldly charm attracted my father in whom she sought a father. Both had surprises coming.

My father was also a copious drinker with a wild temper which my mother describes from time to time in great detail; on the other hand she can be priggish, priding herself on never losing control of herself, or ideally, of others either, a characteristic my father found easy to cite. They were divorced when I was about two, at which time my maternal grandparents came to live with her and me.She returned to work and I saw little of her until I reached puberty. She had many boyfriends who came and went; my grandparents were distant, probably feeling very displaced from their familiar small-town environment. During this period the relationship with my father was the one which left its mark most deeply.

My earliest memory was of lying in a crib and being beaten by an angry, livid face, a man's face, that wielded a stick. For years I have had this image in my mind; for years I have known that my crooked collar bone must have been broken and never set though I remember nothing about it. No feelings, however, were attached to these facts; for years I would look at them and begin to analyze them only to say to myself that I had better stay out of my feelings and my body for fear of some heavy trips that lurked there. At the same time during my life I have been drawn to angry men, and once near them found myself hypnotized by them as if they physically consumed my entire visual and mental fields. By means of the cube I have come to see an angry man's face as only one of the poles of my existence and not the entire field. The earlier impact of this face was to confuse the basis of moral categories: even as an infant I had lost my innocence. I could not cry or need without guilt and terror. The evil old man once again confused moral categories.I could not feel an animating bias coming out of the center of my own personal existence. I could never risk the dreams and ideals only the innocent can feel. I had no center.

In addition my father's identity was kept a secret from me until I was an adolescent. My school career began late in the middle of third grade since the intervening years were spent if not in bed then in the bedroom. On my first day of school I was bombarded with *the* question that comes to those raised in a patriarchal society: "Who are you? Who is your father?" Mentally I was plunged back into the abyss of those years at home, I remember nausea and dizziness from those years with that scalding shame that leaves one feeling red and raw. There were nightmares from which I could not wake up in which the room spun away leaving me cold and alone, only to turn and rush towards me, now feeling hot and sweaty and afraid of being crushed. I eventually learned to concentrate on small objects such as a radiator handle to still the spinning. This whirlwind has followed me for many years in many places.

Recently when the pull of disorientation and isolation was strongest, I have had the cube as an incubator. Inside it the child could survive. I could visit the child and watch it. It banged its head on the walls as I had done as if to confront something stable in its life; the despair I had known turned to pleasure as the banging became brushing the walls with its hair. Preserving the child was very important because when I imagined my way into the cube myself, the opening was at the good young girl apex; that was the corner that was empty. While sitting inside and trying to fill out the corners, *that* one would often seem to blur or sag. Finally an image appeared there of a black girl reading a poem in which she says that she gathers strength from the home folks, she gives the sun its gold. When the cube was finally completed by this image it began to glow itself; so she gave my cube *its* gold too. With her supporting me from below and behind, I gradually began to confront the angry red face in the upper left hand corner facing me. It became a self-contained locus of redness, and no longer with the feelings of being raw and bleeding or scalded and skinless and ashamed. The pole of the angry and hence evil old man no longer overwhelmed the good young girl; for the first time both could have a separate yet complementary existence. As images in a network I could hold them both in my mind without judgement.

If this was the impasse the child had to survive, the next step was that of consciously choosing to confront my body and the feelings that were stored there. I asked the *I Ching* about my descision and received the hexagram of "turning point" or "return." One unbroken line is entering at the bottom of five broken lines. "The time of darkness is past. The winter solstice brings the victory of light." This hexagram sent me back to the cube, in particular to the relation between the two figures evoked by its constituent trigrams: the evil old woman, the witch, on top, the evil old man, the magus, below. These cubal character types, the magus and the witch, unite in a complementary way since the rising energy of the former encounters the down-turning energy of the latter. In terms of my life imagery this represented a first since my mother as witch first of all placed herself beneath my father the evil old man. Then it was she, terrified by his anger, who sued for divorce. For my part this confrontation obliged me to see these characters as part of myself and to participate both in the witch's confusion of identities and the wizard's confusion of moral categories. Whereas I would have liked to keep my father and mother apart from me, I discovered them inside me. Whereas like my mother, I would have simply rejected the angry old man, here I had not only to accept him as part of me, but discover my innocence in the midst of rage. For the first time opposing energies felt complementary.

As I imaginatively returned to the cube, little by little the upper left corner, the residence of the evil old man, began to change. It was counterbalanced by the strength of the good young girl and therefore could no longer dominate the scene; its explosive character became less threatening and moved through images of joyful eruption to end in a large red flower. Finally in my personal life I felt free to express my anger as well as my desire.

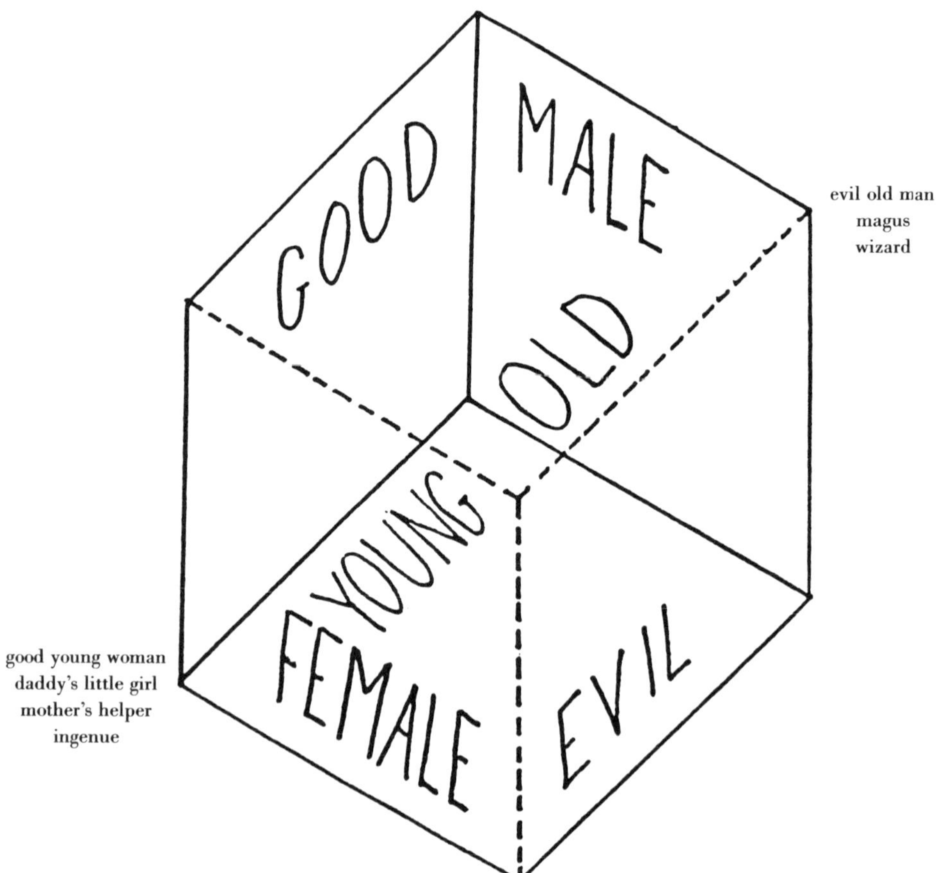

Entry into Switzerland

Moving as a resident into a French-speaking part of the world in my thirties was a crisis in several ways. First of all, up to this time French had been a language of liberation. Freed from the emotional associations that clogged a free use of English, French permitted me to speak about areas of my life which were too anxiety laden to touch in English. Second as a student and teacher of French in the United States I had found a slot for myself where wit and intellect were valued and where I could have a public identity of my own. When I arrived in Switzerland, I discovered that it was not like France at all and that different standards were applied to residents as opposed to tourists. Whereas my efforts in French were complimented in France where I was seen as a temporary asset, in Switzerland where I had become a potentially permanent liability, they met counter efforts to make me more "normal" in a variety of ways. I found myself back in third grade psychologically, confronted by an audience which was making incomprehensible demands on me. In addition, I had no independent identity, but was part of the furnishings of my husband's world. To add insult to injury the wit and intellect which characterize French culture were rather lacking here where they are seen as potential threats to social stability. My living space had suddenly shrunk to the size of a dot in a Weininger-like world.

As was the case for that dot in a nineteenth-century world,the only acceptable role for me was that of Mother, which assailed me with yet another irony. My daughter, whom I had enjoyed mothering was then eight and less dependent than ever. I was interested in exploring other aspects of myself just at the time when social pressures were pushing me into a past that had fulfilled me as past but not as future. I was also caught in the situation of reconstructing "home," and finding my husband more dependent than ever before, whereas my daughter had been liberated by good public transportation and high standards of safety.

While stuck in the mother role, I was also confronted with the negative images I was calling up in others. I wore blue jeans, dressed rather sloppily, sang folk songs in public and went to evening yoga classes, none of which respectable professors' wives do. Activities, interests and life styles that had coexisted with adequate role identity in the States were in conflict with social acceptability here. I was made to feel like a prostitute and as a result began to study the phenomen. If I needed the freedom that was associated with prostitution, then perhaps there is something in it for women in general. Aside from sexual habits, my demand for a public identity, the right to work and the right to compensation for my work was seen as "prostituting" in a village culture where women did not go outside the home. I felt all women had the right to what I wanted, which was essentially the right to one's own goals in a life not circumscribed by other's prerogatives.

My experience as a foreigner made me painfully aware of the relativity of cultural lies. Although we do not create life, we do create the meanings which we see in it and I knew as a stranger that I alone was responsible for my own meanings. Once one has left home there is no going back. I also knew that the figure of the prostitute was capable of giving me access to the *animus* or animating spirit I would need to create the coordinates I needed to live by. The cube would eventually emerge from these efforts.

I followed the "prostitute" as one of my guiding poles. First of all, I found a job teaching English at the United Nations. Here I could have an independent identity and work on my verbal and intellectual skills. Second, I became an editor of *Anima* magazine and began writing about the songs I had been singing, particularly in the light of exploring the Jungian concepts of *anima* and *animus*. In the course of my reading I discovered Esther Harding and her interpretation of ritual prostitution. Here for the first time the meaning for the woman was considered! Whereas contemporary prostitution makes the woman a mirror for the man, temple prostitution reversed the situation. Women passing through this initiation rite or living with it as a profession were asked to remain in a temple sexually available for strangers whom they could not frequent outside of this religious context. The woman then was the bearer of cultural meaning and invited by the unknown quality of the stranger to experience her own *animus* projections, her own masculinity. In doing so she became what Esther Harding would call a true virgin, meaning one who was united with herself. In other societies more recent than that of ancient Greece I learned that the prostitute alone had access to "spirit" as culture as well as self. She alone among women in India for example had access to the arts and to reading and writing. She had a double role of prostitute and of teacher of the arts. Nonetheless even there in a non-Western context her role was definitively separated from that of mother. I however was a mother and now was exploring its same side opposite on the cube.

The particular problem for Western women is to claim for themselves the other side of the two qualities canonized in the myth of the Virgin Mary. In her the innocent virgin unites with the fertile mother, excluding the anger and assertiveness which in cultural encoding compromise innocence and the female sexuality which fell into disrepute with the Fall and has been devalued ever since. In Harding's interpretation of prostitution, however, sexuality is the vehicle by which a woman attains the state of "virginity" which implies the innocence of at-one-ment, of being one's own person. If female sexuality and innocence have to be reunited for the benefit of women, so anger-assertiveness needs to be related to mother's fertility, which, without the former, is of use only to others, primarily men.

The crisis of my entry into Switzerland constellated the polar opposition between the prostitute figure and the wise old man which when resolved restored innocence and understanding to the prostitute and met my deepest need for a supportive father. The prostitute's shape-shifting had shown the link between a compromising sexuality and a promising life of the spirit; one of her messages is that the brain is as much body as the bottom. Jung perhaps implied the same thing when he said that a Western yoga must start in the mind rather than in the body. Psychologist Joe Havens in a similar vein would add a Western fifth yoga to the four from India. By focusing on human "otherness" with its origin in mental concepts of social expectations and roles, it also reverses the Eastern concentration on the body. As we will see later the reentry into Switzerland restored to the mother a healthy anger and assertiveness which break the stereotype of Mother-ever-mindful-of-others.

For the moment I need to introduce the polar figure in counterbalancing tension with the prostitute— the wise old man, the guru whom I encountered with the help of yoga. Although I did meet him in person in Paris this was largely an inner experience. It began when while meditating I saw and heard him: this was in the same spring that my grandfather and my father-in-law died and was a very profound experience. It ended with an image of myself as a sick child with an angry man beside me— a combination which was too frightening for me to cope with. Only recently has this crisis reached resolution as a result of the work done on the prior angry old man—good young girl crisis. Through a guided imagery trip I found home inside myself as my "other" inner woman found love and acceptance at the feet of the wise old man.

Reentry into the United States

Whereas entry into Switzerland made me aware of my helplessness and dependence, reentry into the United States gave me a surge of energy and a feeling of power. As a woman I could call important people without depending on my husband's status or personal connections. People were interested in what I was doing not simply in who my husband was. Within minutes from where we lived I could be on an expressway which would take me anywhere I wanted to go. In a year my husband and I drove over 25,000 miles; in a bit more than a month I wrote my first book. The

good old man
father
guide

evil young woman
prostitute
seductress

intellectual, verbal and psychological skills that had been growing in Switzerland flourished in *Meaning in Star Trek.*

Star Trek was a perfect fit for the animus energies which had been building up. It was a male, masculine and military world, a microcosm of our traditional Western one, with certain important modifications such as the presence of Spock, the alien who rang true to my years as an alien.

Moving back to the States was moving into an energy high which was perhaps constellated in part by the proximity of mother. Just as my father had been the evil old man in my life, so my mother was the evil old woman, the witch. Whereas my father's shape-shifting touched on moral categories, my mother's concerned social categories. Having refused categorically the socially enforced mother script of living for others, she had to survive without the cultural support offered more conventional women. She insisted on living for herself and whereas a man in the same frame of mind would have many cultural tools at his disposal, she had only chaos, the shape-shifting we associate with the witch.

Shape-shifting in fact entered my life early. First of all during the time I was kept home from school sick, a series of mother figures including grandmother, maids and babysitters drifted through my life. My mother did not become apart of my life until I reached early adolescence. As soon as I became sexually attractive, she involved me in her social life as her sister, a situation which posed no internal problems of labelling since I had never been allowed to call anyone "mother", but which did pose identity problems. She also involved me in her work life, alternatively as her sister, her daughter, her cousin or her friend. I was constantly terrified of saying the wrong thing, or letting it be known that I was younger than I said and appeared or that she was older. Her social identity shifted and with it mine; I had no sure orientation and the anxiety of not knowing what was expected of one was my constant companion. In addition there was the continual fear of damaging her scripts, which threatened the whole world.

Not only did she disorient me socially in terms of roles, but also in terms of living space. Her apartment is a catacomb with objects piled everywhere such that one can neither sit nor lie down without dislodging something which in turns threatens to arouse her anger. Her household familiar is a cat which is not housebroken and exhibits its intelligence by vomiting in the presence of strangers. Its smells fill the apartment, serving as territorial warnings and as disorientation devices. Nothing is where it "ought" to be. Her speech is an ongoing linguistic chaos that makes it difficult to think for oneself.

Whereas the Atlantic Ocean had provided a protective distance from her spell, I was now within danger range. I had to rely on myself in her presence since I would be on her territory. The intuitive awareness of other's expectations which I had learned for survival with her could drag me into an unconscious union with her in which I would lose myself. The intellectual skills I had learned in Europe would be greatly needed to compensate for the dangers of too much intuition. Silence in her presence was also a survival technique which would have to be replaced by some kind of self-expression if I were to survive as myself: this again could draw on the verbal skills developed in Europe.

Although she was certainly a witch figure, inherited cultural conceptions concerning mothers and daughters were certainly not going to help me distinguish myself from her. In so far as there is no culturally encouraged principle for female consciousness, there is no acceptable way of separating oneself from the mother either personally or even stereotypically. In my case although nothing is farther from the stereotype of Mother than my mother, I was vulnerable to being manipulated in terms of the former until I learned to separate myself from the latter.

Although much of my mother's energy was directed into manipulating men who continually flowed through her life (and mine when I was with her), none of her relationships were deep and most were based on some falsified identity. The distance was often provided by the age and social status of the man, whom she would refer to even after as long as ten or fifteen years later as Mr.... or Dr....She never dated peers or people younger than she appeared to be. She preferred the father figure or the morally questionable older man, assiduously avoided her polar opposite, the good young man, except when she tried to select a husband for me. It was just those characteristics I had unknowingly embodied through developing my *animus* energy, my good young man.

Confronted by her chaos I created the cube, which is above all a means of organization and a source of conceptional symmetry at least if not as a locus of equality between the sexes. The cube served to reveal inequities which could justify my anger and assertion of individuality. As a tool for external use it functioned admirably to incorporate and to make use of the witch's chaos; as a tool for internal use it functioned equally well to counter the wizard's rage.

Having written *Meaning in Star Trek*, I returned alone to the States as her daughter, unprotected by the activity of writing and interviewing and travelling. This time I took only myself, a camera and a tape recorder. I had the feeling of recreating on my terms a kind of Oedipal ritual for the separation of myself from her. I wanted a means of establishing my identity as distinct from hers which would obviously not be lethal and which would be less guilt laden than that of Oedipus. Since the purpose of it is to keep intact the eyes and the I which can establish a sense of self and of its boundaries, anything guilt provoking would be counterproductive since guilt acts as a hole in one's identity through which the past can continue pouring out its influence. I decided to use tools I consider creative, so I photographed her physical chaos and taped her verbal chaos so that I could distinguish myself from the aura she creates around her and look at her clearly in other contexts with other key character types. The witch has covert powers which gain their force through being unknown to the victims. My mother's chaos is great enough to tap anyone's reservoir of anxiety and to elicit the projections which make them malleable to her ends. Hence my affirmative action was to return to the chaos and bring it to the light of the intellect, and to the service of the good young man who can be as much a part of a woman as of a man once we grasp the functioning and significance of the cube.

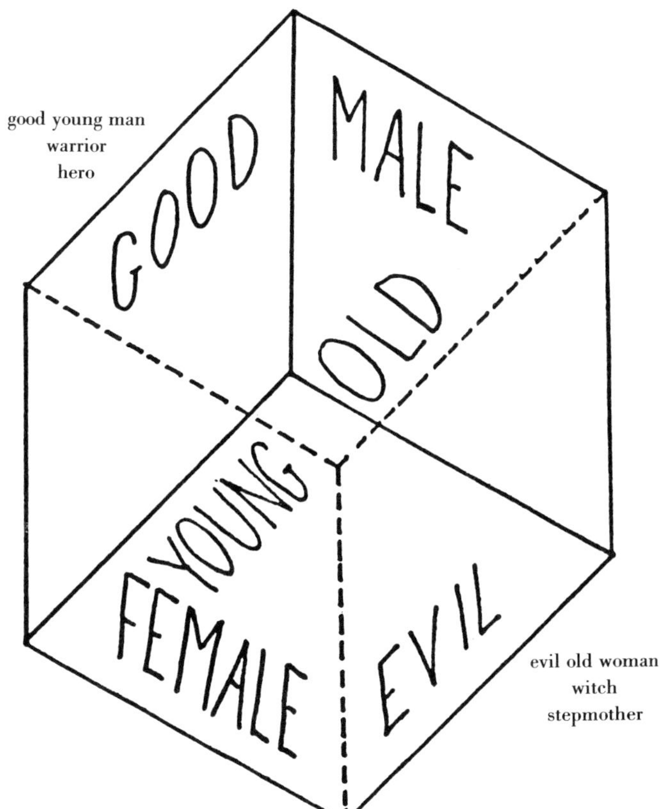

Reentry into Switzerland

On entry into Switzerland my daughter needed less mothering: on the reentry she required none since she remained for two more months in school alone in the States. Just as I was freed from anyone's real need for my mothering, I felt the most stuck in the expectations of the men around me who were calling up mother in every way possible. Just as everyone seemed to want to depend on me, I felt most in need of support.

Stateside it had been doubly easy to be active and analytical, spurred on as I had been by the threat of losing myself in my mother. Now I collapsed into my swamp. I needed a mother; if I had to be one, it would have to be in relation to myself as well as others. However this is the problem: if mothers by definition are concerned only for the needs of others, how can they take care of themselves, since their "self" does not exist really in and of itself, at least in so far as cultural codes are concerned.

At this point "the trickster" entered my life. In addition to the unexpected and increased demands for mothering coming from my husband in whose eyes I was never so free while feeling never so stuck myself, I met an angry young man, complete with black leather jacket and motorcycle. He was both angry and deceptive: he inspired ideas which he never carried out; he made promises he never kept. In every way possible he invited projections. Perhaps in this rejected no man's land of evil figures a kind of natural symmetry can persist such that

trickster:	woman	=	prostitute:	man	and
trickster:	man	=	prostitute:	woman	

Nonetheless the figure of the prostitute must be removed from her stereotypical role of sex object in relation to men. Whereas the prostitute introduces men to their projections by functioning as a mirror, the trickster did that for me. As perfect projection screen, the trickster was promising to be there and leaving me to realize that it was only myself I had for company.

In addition my dream life became as vigorous now as my intellectual life had been in the States. A recurring theme was that of birth, thus constellating the mother figure, the polar opposite of the trickster. Then an issue of *Spring*[2] came which had synchronic significance for me. The two lead articles were on dreams of cancer patients which it turned out often included birth imagery, but skewed, gone awry, as when, for example, a woman gives birth to seaweed out of her back, the future locus of her cancer. I felt lucky. My dream of birth had been of a healthy baby and I was ten years younger than the woman about whom the article was written. Yet I believed that if I did not give birth to this in me, myself, whatever it was, I too would have cancer in ten years. Cancer was seen as a kind of unwilling sacrifice to the gods of life. Its symptoms could have been transformed into symbols had one engaged one's consciousness in the process. The root of "symbol" means that which is thrown together, implying aim and intention; those of "symptom" that which falls together. Disease in this perspective was a failed response to a crisis of one's creativity. I was in such a crisis.

As I had separated myself from my personal mother now I had to separate myself from the stereotypical mother. I had to find in myself that aim and intention, that conscious will which could create symbols. I needed my masculine consciousness to tell me not only who I was not, i.e. that I was different from both my personal mother and maternal stereotypes, but more importantly who I was. At the same time I had to nurture that new being. I had to be both good old woman and bad young man, mother and trickster who was tricking me right then with the idea that he was different from me and opposed to the mother, his polar opposite.

My writing and intellectual work was involving me in a continuation of the research done in the States on women's studies and women's roles. My cube was still seen as a device to justify a woman's anger at the social situation. I was finding myself in an impasse, at a point at which there are no models for women as individuals with goals of their own. My anger may have been justified, but I needed it to function creatively. For a while my anger stayed on paper. Motherhood had been totally appropriated by the male establishment, both physically in so far as physicians took over the birth process, psychologists the developmental process and the male shape makers those cultural molds into which all children must fit. Women provided the raw material. I felt raw, flayed, skinless. Mothers exist only for others; but if I was to give birth to myself in some way I had to know who I was. I had to be someone in and of myself. While I had been "really" mothering my daughter and coping somehow with the social role, I had been cultivating my inner male energy, which was what had created the cube which now seemed so irrelevant to my aching need for touching, mothering.

I felt like an open wound until one day, the day of Assumption of the Virgin, my anger welled up from the inside. I went on a trip to the Loetschental to watch a pre-Christian celebration in which the villagers wear huge grotesque masks. It was the trickster's idea and, of course, he never showed up. I went with some other people and discovered that the inhabitants of the valley were not present either. While they were hiding their celebration, tourists like ourselves were looking for them; however, there was no lack of everyday masks to be seen as one walked in the mountains. One of the women I went with told us that she had just buried her mother who began to hemorrhage while changing the bandage on a leg ulcer. My companion's father who was with his wife continued to bring bowls to catch the blood she would have had to clean up had she not bled to death. Now my friend wondered how her poor old father would survive without her mother to care for him.

Twice tricked by the events of the day my anger rose up like the Virgin to heaven and my wound began to scab over. I was about to bleed to death into someone else's bowls, masks, expectations, formulations. I began to be able to mother myself, at least enough to survive. Little did I know then how the cube was later to intervene as needed incubator in the process of giving birth to this self that has a skin and body boundaries as well as an ego and social boundaries, that is able to counter both an angry old man's rage with its own anger and innocence and a witch's chaos with its own structure. Little did I know how much I needed to learn from the trickster that what I saw in him were my projections just as what he saw in me—mother—were his projections.

The affirming activity for this polar crisis resolution has been the recent ability to shape shift for others. I have consciously tried to incorporate the trickster's techniques but have only very recently been able to be aware of others' expectations for me and at the same time aware of the fact that I am under no obligation to fulfill them and able to risk the potential confrontation of not always doing what I "should." At last I could combine the intuitive awareness of the scripts others are writing that include me with my own freedom.

Ending the women's group in fact necessitated the use of this newly found part of myself. Cast once again in the role of mother I was able to understand the situation and given only what I could give from within me rather than feel obligated to fulfill the mother-role expectations. Once again I was forced to realize that there are no precedents for separating a daughter's consciousness from a mothering role. It is in fact as difficult to do so in relation to women's expectations as it is in relation to men's. In this perspective I see in the women's movement a tendency to skirt this essential issue of being oneself by relying on communal activity and on the group for identity. Whereas the group could serve as needed transitional space, it fails its potential when it becomes as end in itself. Whereas men dominate by imposing their ego demands on others or by asking others to identify with them, women dominate by blurring the ego boundaries which still are necessary to individual life as we know it. The ultimate challenge is to live on the creative edge of oneself with enough chaos within to create new worlds without. The ego is necessary to resolve the creative crisis into symbols rather than symptoms.

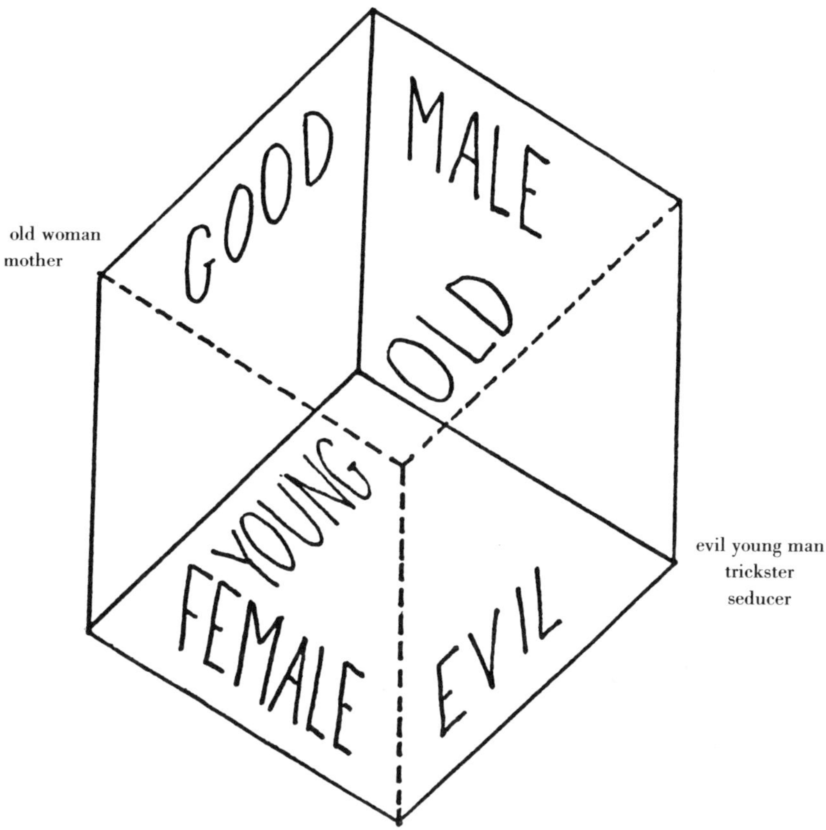

Notes to Chapter 2

1. Harding, p. 221.
2. Russell A. Lockhart, "Cancer in Myth and Dream," *Spring* 1977, pp. 6-7.

3
Conclusion

This study has included diverse material in hopes of creating an in-depth perspective on the functioning of the cube as a conceptual matrix. From Martin Gardener and mathematics through Edward Albee and plays we have moved from Weininger and turn-of-the-century moral philosophy through the psychological models of Freud, Jung and Perls, to the *I Ching* with its complementary Eastern perspective. Then from Part I, which by itself would lack concreteness and practical human relevance, we have moved in Part II to the personal experience of a group of foreign women living in Geneva and finally my own experience with the cube. Without the first part the latter would have lacked structure; without the cube my personal experience and that of others might seem chaotic whereas with the cube chaos itself acquires a place in a structure.

The importance of a conceptual structure as complete as the cube is considerable if one takes seriously the psychological principle that striving after any goal or ideal constellates its opposite. In this perspective those figures which display only power such as the traditional good father as physician or priest or teacher do not invite the "others," the patient, the lay person or the pupil to take part in their own development. On the other hand acknowledged weakness in the healer can engage the healing powers of the patient. The union of these opposing forces brings growth. Similarly

> Both ego and collective ideals must be repeatedly subject to attack since they are false and onesided. Were they not continually being eaten into from the depth of the human soul, there would be neither individual nor collective development.[1]

Growth then results from the complementary interaction of opposing forces. Society establishes a number of power-polarized pairs such as teacher-student, physician-patient, priest-parishioner, parent-child. In each of these pairings there is a superior and a subordinate position with the role of the former being to raise that of the latter to a condition of equal at least in the sense of co-human. The goal of teaching students is to educate them and make them perhaps teachers themselves one day, the goal of the doctor is to heal the patient who will no longer be dependent, the goal of the priest is to nourish the moral and spiritual lives of the parishioners, the goal of the parent is to raise the child to independence and perhaps to parenthood one day. As *Power in The Helping Professions* suggests, in so far as power constellates its opposite, the unilateral claim to power by the socially designated superiors calls forth only more weakness in those who are already needy. Open expression of weakness can on the other hand stimulate inner power in the other and hence energy and growth.

In sexual terms, these notions have strong implications, as have been touched upon at several points. The relationship between men and women has been socially established as one of male superiority relating to female dependence and subordination. However, in this case alone, as far as I know, there is no socially codified process of development understood to be part of the inequal distribution of power. While doctors do go to other doctors as patients and priests go to other priests for confession and teachers go to school as students, men have no social slot in which to display their femininity, their dependency. Men are not given their power in order to train women to share it. Male power is thought to be inherent in them just as female weakness is a "natural" trait. This power structure would in fact be threatened if a man displayed weakness—femininity vis-a-vis a woman whose personal power—masculinity—might then emerge. Or to put it a bit differently any structure which does not give every man and every woman rounded access to identity with the characterisitcs of the opposite sex serves to maintain an unequal distribution of power. The absence of such symmetrical models in our society perhaps lies at the bottom of the crises which women are now facing when confronted with demands for change. The search is a double one, for models of positive female strength on the hand and for acceptable male weakness on the other. Weakness must include the very positive forces of sympathy, kindness, nurture which have traditionally made men "effeminate," but which might actually make them more human if not humane.

In this perspective the crises constellated in me by culture change seem to be microcosms of the changes going on among many women and men since change in one affects the other. The catalyzing agent in my experience was the stranger which I was to others when I changed cultures and which others were to me. Although I had often said I felt like a stranger even before making a cross-cultural move those feelings were still in a context of familiarity. To confront the stranger outside such a context is a different experience. The potency of the stranger is implicit in Esther Harding's interpretation of ritual prostitution. Traditionally speaking the prostitute was the priestess with whom the stranger would unite for the betterment of his soul. However, Harding chose to see the ritual in terms of the prostitutes' perspective partly perhaps because she was a woman, but more so I feel because of the potency of the stranger as projection screen. Whereas the prostitute as priestess was part of known socio-religious canons the stranger was an open space, a true projection screen, an unknown, or part-known. As part-unknown (part-culture, part-nature) he more than she was part of the entire world of dieties which are hybrid creations.

The stranger as if by virtue of this half-and-half construction invites entry into one's other half. The experience of one's "bad" side can be creative when it is not felt as a catastrophe script. As one of many states to be experienced it is a condition of growth. Thus the function of hospitality rituals traditionally kept it within a religious context. Culture change like religion was until recently limited to men, which contributed to the dearth of models for undergoing this experience that led me to the cube. I needed a context within which to structure and understand these experiences which threatened to overwhelm me. I needed a way to relate to a bad side I felt I needed though others scorned it. I also had a very deep spiritual hunger. However I had to explore all the dimensions of my psycho-social space before I could move with it, to intersect the energy field, the stream of life, the unknown, whatever one wishes to call it. All corners of the cube, my die, have to be present before it can be cast.

This study, which was begun in frustration and anger at the apparent impossibility of ever breaking out of the prison of skewed social role and personal chaos ends in joy. The cube which began conceived as a kind of club or weapon held my inner child when it needed an incubator to gain strength to go through the impasse, the sick point. From prison it then became a prism through which I could use my mind to enlighten, not overrule, my life experience. Now I feel I have a set of coordinates by which to see where I am and to judge the equity of the possibilities afforded by the environment. The cube is a map, but it is also a road, as such it has brought me into contact with my experience and that of others around me. Regardless of wider meanings such conact has its own value and its own reward.

Writing the study was itself an experience of opposition. As my mind was working the hardest, beneath the surface was another layer of imagery preparing to surface. As I was dealing with the imagery, another intellectual step was being set up. Thus the relationship between two parts is one of continuous co-operation without which neither would have been finished.

Above all what was begun in anger at Switzerland ends in gratitude. First of all had I remained in the States, a variety of factors, starting with familiar social codes and ending with familiar TV shows, might have helped a "natural" i.e. culturally trained, tendency to avoid my "bad" side. I would have known how to fulfill superficially my needs without ever really having to cope with crossing lines of social expectations. I would have been able to see each evening some favorite TV characters act out my "other" selves so that I would never have to confront them and accept them as my own. I would have known how to remain in "friendly" surroundings compared to the apparently gratuitous projections one gives and receives as a stranger. However, I would not have been able to have the fuller sense of self and of what it is to be human that entering and reentering Switzerland has permitted me.

For the many fortuitous conjunctions of people, need, situation which has brought the cube about and which the cube has brought about I can only be grateful. The following section uses the cube as die and cubal dice, to move from reflecting on culture change to encountering the unpredictable.

Notes to Conclusion

1. Adolph Guggenbuhl-Craig, *Power in The Helping Professions* (New York: Spring, 1971), p. 123.
2. Guggenbuhl-Craig, p. 113.

Part III

Only where love and need are one
And the work is play for mortal stakes,
Is the deed ever really done
For Heaven and the future's sakes

Robert Frost

Introduction

Although I needed time to digest the incubation going on in me, I nonetheless had to cope with the others met in everyday life. I needed to relate fictionalizing the people I *had* met to the unknown others I was still to meet. The question was how could I make the link. Reflecting on this problem, I finally stumbled on the octahedron as a correlative of the cube when used as a die. And so I moved into the realm of play as a way to bridge the gap between cubal analysis and human needs. The resulting pages reflect areas in which I have moved by means of the die. Rather than reflections on or fictionalizations of experience they present techniques for cubal analysis of anyone's life situation.

1
Cubal Analysis and Plane Romance

Once upon a time there was a box that had many-colored sides to go with its multifaced personality. There was a green side where the feminine types admired the growth of grass and leaves and plants of all kinds. Some saw swampy marshes as well as growth.

Opposite that was a bright red side where the he-men preened their vigor while adjusting their ski caps. Some saw anger there as well as energy.

Then there was the dark blue side which was deep like the sky at night. Old people saw themselves there, and found reflection in its glimmering stars.

Youth came to the yellow side to admire the eternal sun, the golden lights, that unchanging fostered growth.

There was also a white side where the innocent would peer in self-admiration.

The black side was always on the bottom.

The cube felt very full and complete with so many people coming to see themselves in its sides, but they only came to look at their favorite side and always saw the same thing. They never spoke to one another about what they saw to avoid arguments: how could the greens ever see red without compromising themselves. No one ever stayed long since each knew just what to look for. Little by little the cube felt lonely. No one ever appreciated its many dimensions. Also, while others could come and go, it just stayed in the same place.

But the little box consoled itself. "At least I'm not one-sided even if I can't move".

One day after the daily visitors had gone it tried to move. It got itself all on edge: it suddenly became aware of its black bottom. No one will want to see themselves in that: I'll just be more lonely".

And so it lay there.

Blocked.

While many faces came and went, flexing muscles, primping hair, preening moral fiber, comparing symptoms, complaining about parents.

If it turned over a new leaf, it would not only show its black bottom, but would black out one group of these familiar faces.

Time passed.

Eventually some of the golden young men came to explore the blue sky—they came resigned, as if once blue no other color was possible.

The cube felt sorry for them. It also noticed how even the yellow-siders seemed resigned in their way. Sometimes they seemed tired of glitter or tired of numbness by the continuity of the color.

How, the cube wondered, could it show the visitors that the other colors are possible? Where, the cube wondered, could more colors come from? So that some blue, for example, might be visible even on the yellow side.

In despair of helping its visitors, the cube lay down and discovered itself in the black bottom. It fell asleep and dreamt that out of the black came all colors.

When the cube awoke, it was so happy that it wanted to tell everyone about its dream. It struggled and struggled with itself going from one edge to the other. Its fellow cubes we e amused with its instability. "You're ruining our arrangement" they told it."You think you've seen something new, but black is nothing". "What if someone saw your black bottom, think of the disgrace..."

The poor cube was more alone than ever. but it kept trying clumsily to roll around and balance longer and longer on edge, little by little getting used to this kind of uneasy feeling.

It learned to balance on its edges, where two colors could come together and one day it realized it had even a tiny space where three colors could come together.

Just to make a point it strained and slipped and poised itself for a moment's perfect balance. Right there time seemed to hang as on a thread. People could then see all three dimensions: young or old, male or female, good or bad.

As it tottered there unwilling to settle for any double-edged compromise, an octahedron came by. It was much impressed by the efforts of what had always seemed to be a lower species. Seeing the block now from a new angle, it realized what a perfect couple they could make together.

The octahedron rolled gallantly over with wide-angled largesse and embraced the tottering cube.

Now men and women can get together and young and old and good and bad—and all the colors can mingle.

The visitors were annoyed at first. "Where's my color?" they demanded indignantly. But looking harder they could glimpse it here and there. Yet whatever they sought looked different, surrounded by other colors they had never seen before. Nonetheless each was determined to find himself or herself and continued searching in a many-colored maze. And little by little annoyance turned into amazement: they realized how many different colors there were to see themselves through. Finally they learned to see through the limits of monochrome.

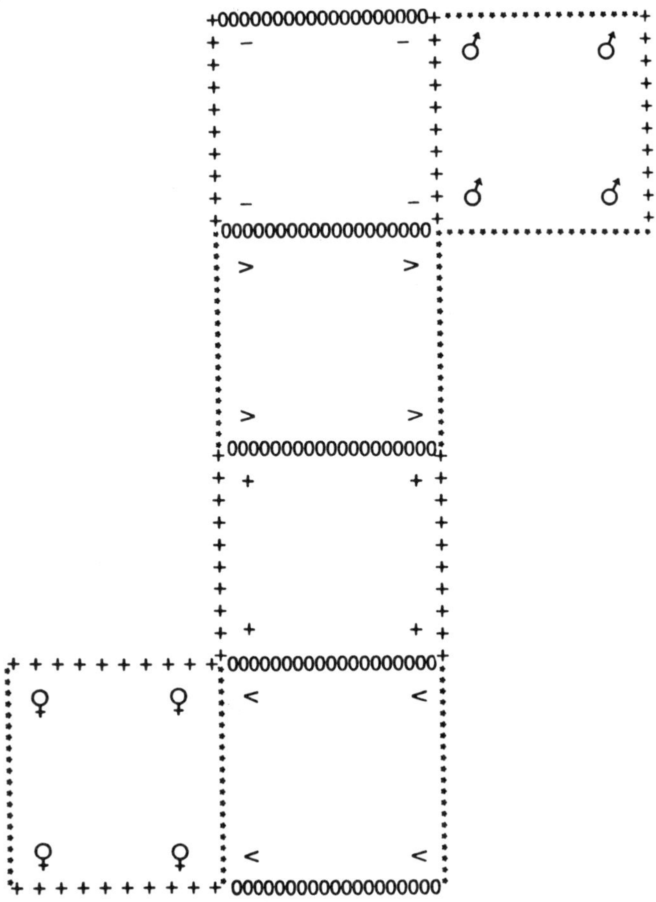

Using these as models you can make your own cubes and octahedrons.

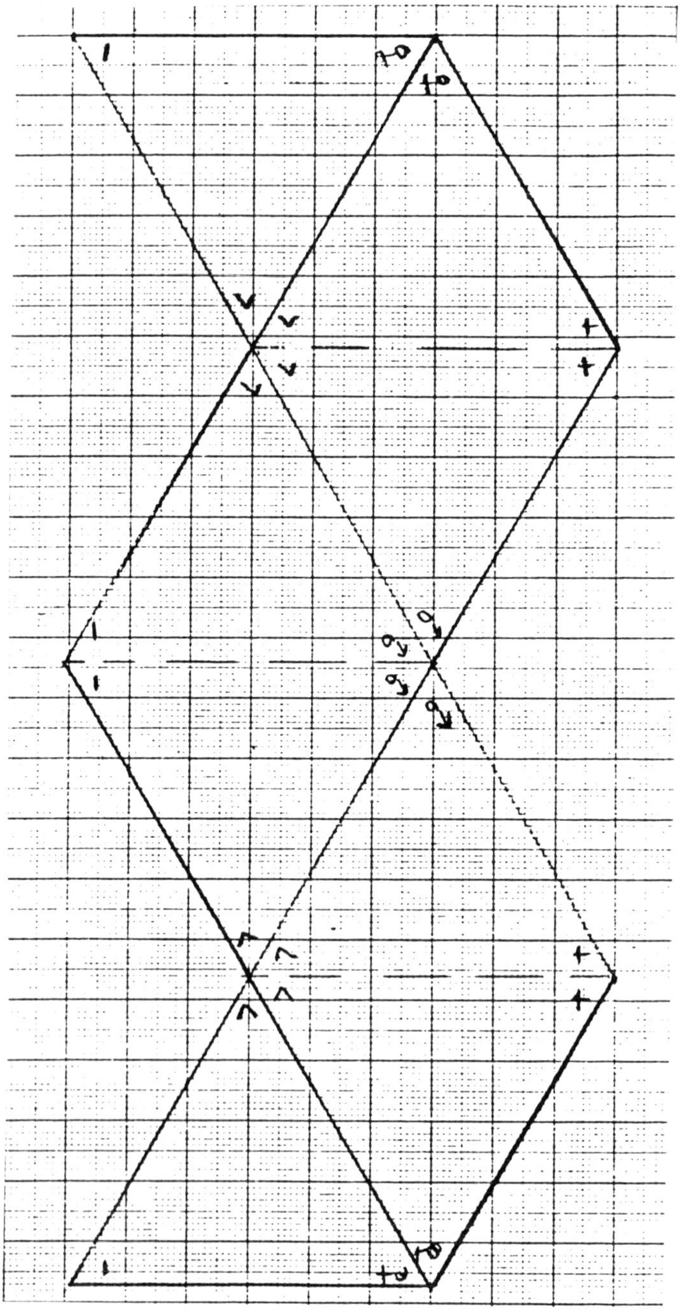

2
Cubal Analysis as a Basis for Gaming

As an analytical tool the cube's eight apexes offered images for psychic polarities. As a three dimensional object the cube when rolled as a die could only offer one face: one team of each of three pairs involved in elaborating the cube as analytical tool. The surface representing either youth or age would lie face up, or that representing male or female, or that representing good or evil would be the only one on top. The octahedron, however, offers six opposing apexes corresponding to the surfaces of the cube and eight surfaces which correspond to the apexes of the cube. As an object with which one can play the octahedron represents an accessible version of the cube, a play on the cube.

For analysis abstract symbols likewise are functional: " ♂ " and " ♀ " served as shorthand for male and female, "+" and "-" for good and bad, " > " and " < " for young and old. However, for an individual who was involved in a game rather than in reading and analysing, colors seemed more appropriate than symbols while remaining equally meaningful. Red and green seemed intuitively right to represent male and female, the firey father in the heavens and the verdant mother earth. similarly blue, and yellow seemed perfect symbolizations of age and youth, of night as the end of a day or a life and of sun as the beginning of a day or a life. Black and white as representations of evil and good need no introduction. Thus each surface of the cube as object carries one of these colors with the opposite color being on the opposite surface and each apex of the octahedron carries one of these colors with its opposite or complementary color being on the opposite apex.

The use of these objects, plus the tetrahedron which will be described later, share the basic assumption of the *I Ching*: meaning is not only casual but synchronous. The coming together of all those elements which go into any given moment are mutually meaningful; therefore throwing the *I Ching* or the cube or the octahedron or the tetrahedron will reveal to the thrower something about him or herself at that given time and place.

A use I have made of the cube as fantasized or realized object is for meditation. One can throw the cube and take the color of the exposed surface as a symbol of the qualities and or the quality itself on which to meditate. One can continue to imagine oneself meditating in a cube with the one color of the exposed surface in front of one and the others arranged around one in their appropriate order. A further elaboration is to consciously visit each of the apexes and the psychic polarities they represent while welcoming into oneself all of these diverse qualities and/or people which are invited to flow through one's mind. For me personally such meditations have frequently signalled their own conclusion when the cube begins to glow like gold. Moving mentally between opposites often helps one see their interrelations and appreciate positive qualities in that which has been seen only as "negative", i.e. in terms of lack of the positive element: evil as the absence of good, the feminine as a lack of the masculine and age as the waning of youth. Similarly the cube as meditative device can help one "face" a person who has been a problem in one's life or imagination. Whatever the threat posed by such a person, whether imagined or real, the cube permits it to be conceived in a network of relationships which strengthen the meditator and help him or her keep the threat in perspective. In addition by conceiving the "opposition" as an attribute of continua extending between poles the threat of getting stuck in absolutes is diminished in favor of graduations and coordinates.

3
Cubal Analysis and Meditation

Sit comfortably. Imagine yourself inside a cube as close to the center as possible. Under you is the rising energy of youth, above you the protective energy of age; to your right is the compensatory (to right-handed persons, for example) energy of the feminine, to the left that of the masculine; squarely in front of you is the dimension of "evil" and behind you is that of "goodness." If no images come, one can begin by "dressing" the abstract framework with the colors corresponding to the different qualities. One can then focus on the one which draws most attention. One can consciously visit the different apexes while welcoming into oneself all of the diverse qualities and/or people which are invited to flow through one's mind. A problem area can be indicated by a felt threat or by a blank. The former can be countered by the network of the cube. Whatever the threatening person or event the cube permits it to be conceived in a network of relationships which strengthen the meditator and let the threat be kept in perspective. A blank can similarly be approached through the network provided by the cube. If, for example, one cannot imagine a "good little girl" one can imagine other characters on the other apexes until there is someone who is associated with a good little girl and through whom the "leak" in the cube can be filled.

Whereas the cube as die permitted one to begin by focussing on a color/quality, the octahedron as die exposes a conjunction of three qualities crystallizing a character type: the good old man, the good old woman, the bad old man, the bad old woman, the good young man, the good young woman, the bad young man, the bad young woman. As we saw earlier, the *I Ching* can be arranged to correspond to these apexes. The following chart and game will let you apply the cube and the octahedronal cubal die to the use of the *I Ching*.

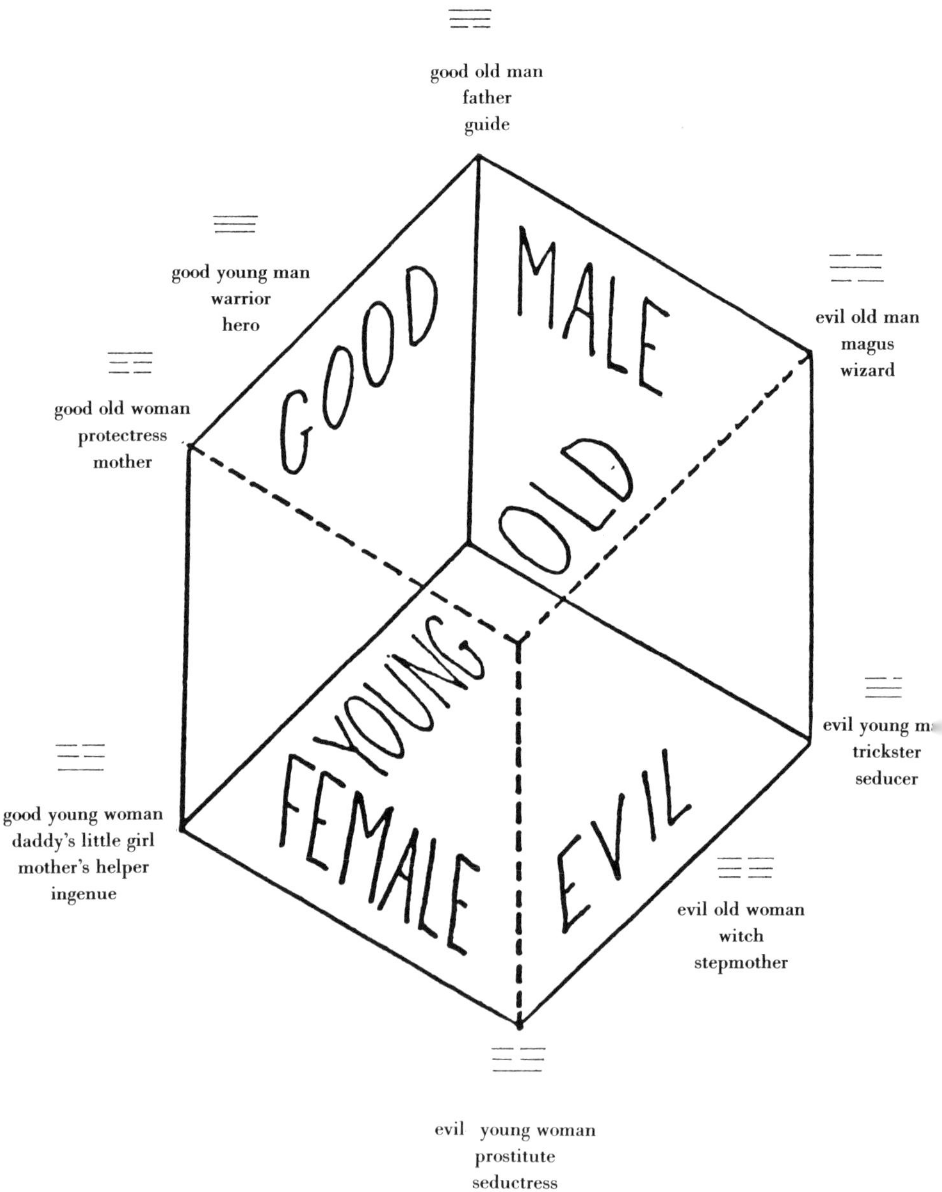
good old man
father
guide
good young man
warrior
hero
good old woman
protectress
mother
evil old man
magus
wizard
GOOD
MALE
OLD
YOUNG
FEMALE
EVIL
evil young
trickster
seducer
good young woman
daddy's little girl
mother's helper
ingenue
evil old woman
witch
stepmother
evil young woman
prostitute
seductress

4
Cubal Analysis and The *I Ching*

As one can see from the diagrams, each apex of the cube corresponds to a surface of the octahedron. Thus each trigram of the *I Ching* which is located on an apex of the cubal die. Continuing with the image of waves as symbolizing the underlying sense of unending change in the *I Ching*, one can take two cubal dice and color one red and the other purple for the two ends of the spectrum. By putting one trigram on each surface of each die, one can throw the two dice and have a relationship between the characters and characteristics of the two trigrams represented. In this way one can make simultaneous use of the western archetypes and the eastern symbolism.

By taking six dice and coloring them in the six colors of the spectrum: red, orange, yellow, green, blue, violet, and then by putting on each surface a weak or strong yin or yang line one can create a situation in which one throw will result in a hexagram with changing lines and with the same probability scale as one would have with the sticks. Each cubal die will have one six (→ ←), one nine (←→), one eight (— —) and one seven (——). The advantage of having the hexagram with one gesture has to do with the process of projection which also happens all at once and not sequentially. When one uses the coins or the sticks one has on the one hand time to reflect, but on the other hand time to try and guess what the hexagram will be. The latter process interferes with the use of the *I Ching* in my experience. By starting with the densest color, the red, one builds the hexagram out of the rainbow components resulting from the throw.

5
Cubal Analysis and Story Telling

One can ask a person to throw the die and tell a story about the character type in question. At this point there are three options: one can ask the person to tell a story using the third person, one can ask the person to take the part of the character type involved, one can ask the person to talk to that character as if it were part of himself. If one is in a group one can ask persons to pair up and either narrate a story about their pair of characters or take the part of their characters and enter into dialogue. In addition having an assortment of photos of people permits one to help the person by offering them as imaginative stimuli: s/he can choose the picture which seems to capture the essence of the character type.

If the context permits one to recycle back to the person insights gained through the story, one can proceed in two ways. When there is total blockage, turning the octahedron to its opposite face will often reveal the source of the problem and permit progress. More frequently, however, there is simply confusion in terms of one or two of the qualities involved. If, for example, one were confronted by a story told by a young man, about a bad young man in which the man does nothing wrong but is victimized by others, one would feel there to be trouble in the area of the morality and guilt. One could then ask the person to turn the cube to the face which best represents those who are the victimizers and ask for another story about them or one could throw the tetrahedronal dice which concentrates attention on one set of opposing terms.

Tetrahedronal dice come in pairs. One of each pair is the exclusive carrier of one term of an opposition., its pair is the exclusive carrier of the other term: all of the other characteristics are equally disturbed. One can choose that pair which involves a troublesome opposition either for oneself or for another. These dice then are especially well adapted to follow through an interpersonal exploration. The non-troublesome characteristics have an equal chance of emerging: the troublesome ones are guaranteed to emerge in opposition. By their asking for a story about the character types which emerge, one asks the person to try to distinguish differences in an area of confusion. One can throw the given pair of dice several times if necessary or move to a meditation on the quality that is giving trouble, or better yet on its opposite. If one gets stuck on the tetrahedronal dice, one can move to the hexahedronal.

6
Cubal Analysis/Gaming

In confronting Cubal Analysis as a game, to play, it makes sense to start with only one cubal option at a time. Any given throw of the die results in one surface on the top and one on the bottom. Here the randomizing factor of the die replaces once again culturally skewed perspectives of our real lives; though one can see this random event as impersonal, it is also possible to see it as in some way significantly connected to one's inner state— the throw then emerges as a kind of index to oneself at this particular time and place. In so far as my presence is not irrelevant to what happens around me, I in some way psychify my surroundings. Thus while in principle the cubal world has parameters which are equally available at any given exposure, in practice there is a specific aspect which reveals itself as a personalized invitation to projection. Without access to all the parameters one might well feel cheated out of some of life's possibilities, yet without the specific case one has nothing to work on; without the specificity of oneself no decisions can be made. Without acknowledging the limits of oneself past decisions become fixations and again no creative movement can be made.

> Two roads diverged in a yellow wood,
> And sorry I could not travel both
> And be one traveller, long I stood
> And looked down one as far as I could
> To where it bent in the undergrowth;
>
> Robert Frost, "The Road Not Taken"

In the same spirit, cubal gaming analysis invites one to contact in imagination parts of oneself which real life culture asymmetries may have suppressed; whereas the cubal model is based on mathematical completeness, the cubal game functions by means of the randomizing die, which produces the relevant individual case.

7

Cubal Analysis/Gaming for Decision Making

Since any terms able to be conceived of through "more" and "less" can be placed on continua, Cubal Analysis lends itself to decision making. By having three axes, the cubal die obliges us to deal with issues in terms of three, which discourages one from endless circles of yes/no, either/or thinking. Decision making is not just a question of "will I do this or that," rather it first of all involves the isolation of the different elements in a situation. Cubal Analysis as an intellectual framework provides guidelines here: in any given situation there are the elements of time, space and social setting. In one set of terms these translate as age, sex, and morality; in another vocabulary they become the intellectual, the physical and the emotional (social interaction); or again the intellectual or structural, the personal and the social. In terms of language these could correspond to questions of register/nuance (personal intention), questions of meaning (socially agreed upon conventions) and grammatical structures.

The first step then of cubal gaming in a decision making context asks that the individual get out of the trap of either/or thinking first by replacing that with continua and second by isolating three elements in the situation which have "more" and "less" aspects The second step of throwing the die introduces the element of randomness as a personalized invitation to reflection. Having imaginatively embraced all the mathematically possible conjunctions of factors we are asked to relate personally to the one we throw. We might find it is just right—or just wrong. But we will find something and therefore break out of the vicious circling that often thwarts decision making.

When having to reach a group decision one can use the same technique as it invites sharing without the problems of an authority figure imposing anything, even the alternatives to be questioned. Consensus can emerge from apparent coincidence: why did half the group throw the same alternative? Sharing reactions to the throws of oneself and others is more fruitful than sharing reactions to oneself and others.

8
Cubal Die for Decision Making

Since the octahedron asks that one have three issues relating to the decision-making situation in terms of "more" and "less", I have chosen to color the poles with more or less intense shades of the three primary colors: red, yellow and blue.

As one sorts out the three primary issues in the situation involved, one gives them a primary color. As one identifies each issue in terms of its "more" and "less" manifestation, one links each pole with the corresponding "more" and "less" intense shade of the color chosen for that issue. In this way the form and color of the die and the surface thrown can be aids in conceiving of the situation. One can continue in this direction by free associating with the colors of the surface thrown: one's associations with red might throw light on why one chose red for the issue associated with it, for example. One's associations with pink (or less intense red) might be quite different from those with red and might permit a different perspective on the same issue seen in a less intense light.

9
Cubal Gaming/Analysis
A Motivational Tool for Teaching

In teaching, one of the profession's chief problems is motivating students to find links between themselves and the content of a given course—an abstract prestructured body of material which a given culture values enough to pass on to new generations. By definition this received material is representative of any given culture's particular adult bias; in addition, by virtue of being prepackaged at least for pedagogical purposes, it appears closed. Neither of these factors invites relationship and frequently hinders students' motivation. The problem then of involving students could be framed in terms of creating an appropriate opening in an apparently closed and arbitrary world they as adolescents have done nothing to make. Thus adolescents seem vulnerable to the conflicting feelings of resenting imposed material while fearing too much freedom. A fruitful balance, the educating encounter, is what we as teachers seek to arrange; total openness, like total closure, invites madness. We need both a non-threatening, non-judgemental structure to give shape and space within which to project our meanings, ourselves.

In terms of teaching a foreign language the material to be learned may easily strike students as remarkably uninviting and closed. It is hard to imagine classroom work less engaging than grammar exercises based on the binary theory of language; i.e., the notion that all language is a manipulation of a two-part system—subject and predicate. Beginning from this abstract principle, then, the simplest transformation is the yes/no question; it is also the least engaging for it invites continuous recycling within a closed and known world. "Is this a pen?" "Yes, it is a pen." "No, it is not a pen." Question words on the other hand are openers which invite involvement and orientation by opening into the unknown: who, why, what, where, when, all point to absences, gaps which therefore offer a variety of possiblities to the potential "gap-filler." "What" obviously needs to be supplied beforehand with possible responses.

"Why" is certainly not a question for Day I; "who," on the other hand, is: "Who am I," "Who are you" are questions one can begin (and end) with.

At this relatively elementary level the cubal die can be useful by calling forth particular idealized character types for imaginative encounter. The teacher can throw it and then invite questions and answers from the students to flesh out the character type which has been rolled. "When was s/he born?" "What does she look like?" "What does she do?" "Where does she live?" "Why is s/he good and/or bad?" are possible questions which can result in a group imagining a rounded human being. This use of the cube permits the teacher to maintain a central position in the classroom while diminishing the aspect of his or her role that imposes material on the students. Introducing the element of chance has always increased student interest and attention.

When the students can work more independently in English, they can be divided into groups of three. One person could throw a die, another could ask questions about his or her image of the character type and the third could write down the resulting description. These roles can be rotated so that each gets the experience of being questioner, answerer and "scribe."

In this situation the level of the students' English is a primary structuring element although even rudimentary questions and answers can be used to explore a character type and bring a new version of it into existence.

At a more advanced level the teacher can choose a situation which invites the use of certain grammatical structures being studied and within that context invite the students to throw the die and respond to the situation in terms of the character type rolled.

The die can also be used as a randomizing factor in any situation: how would a given character type behave in a restaurant, at a station, etc. In a similar way, it is an obvious invitation to role playing: two or more students can take the roles of the characters they throw and create a skit, a dialogue or story. In a group or alone there are three options for structuring a relationship with the character type: one can assume the role oneself, one can address the character and act out the roles in relation to each other, or one can tell a story about the character in the third person.

Another option when role playing is involved is to have students alone or in small groups act out their roles and have the rest of the class guess who they are, what they are doing.

Role playing often raises the question of whether or not this activity involves psychological risks. The assumption of the question seems to be that people want to know themselves and will be attracted to an opportunity to explore their psyches by means of role playing. In fact the opposite seems truer: people will on the contrary go to great lengths to avoid confrontation with themselves and in fact the role of a psychiatrist is often to push the individual in the direction of greater self-exposure and self-knowledge when these are desirable in terms of the individual's goals or life situation. In the classroom situation students are not obliged to reveal themselves more than they wish; thus each one remains in control of the depth of psychic engagement involved.

Gaming also raises the issue of the significance of the random: is synchronicity a connecting principle which competes with traditional causality? Whatever their ultimate "truth," the relevance of synchronicity or of the random as an invitation to participation is practically important. To seek to interpret its significance is to close off some of its possibilities and perhaps to reduce its effectiveness as an invitation to individual participiptation in a given situation. There needs to be an opening extended to students before there can be participiptation.

In relation to fiction the die can also be used as a randomizing factor. For example, at crucial turning points in the plot of a given novel, one can stop the class, throw the die and hypothesize on the evolution of the plot were the character thrown to intervene. For each type one can create a series of alternatives which s/he might provoke or do and ask students to choose which option seems most likely. After going on to read how in fact the novel does proceed, one can look back and discuss the plausibility of the options which were raised.

All games and perhaps all ideas are based on some model of reality. The model underlying Cubal Analysis/Gaming is mathematical and therefore free of cultural bias. This seems to be an important element when dealing with adolescents whose needs include a great deal of exploration before having to take a position in society. It not only permits individualized mental work on the part of the student but also invites individualized group work to proceed in the classroom. Synchronicity can be translated in practical terms into simultanity, which permits more activity per student per hour while at the same time keeping it within a common matrix so that sharing among the groups is both possible and interesting.

Another unexpected impact of Cubal Analysis/Gaming is that its structures invite adolescents to relativize polar opposites often taken to be absolute contraries: questions of age, gender and morality can be seen as locatable on each axis as a continuum. Thus rather than an absolute dichotomy between male and female or young and old, the opposites can be seen as interrelating, perhaps even as interpenetrating. Even the good/bad of culture-specific moral judgement can be seen with the same sort of relativity that seems natural to us all in terms of the here/there of space distinctions and the then/now of time. In short, this aspect of Cubal Analysis/Gaming could contribute to ease the all-or-nothing at all tendencies of adolescents in crisis.

10
Cubal Analysis and Crises

Crises are not peculiar to adolescents. Rather they seem to characterize for some frequent passages in life and for others only those times of especially difficult changes. In the most elementary terms crises could be defined as a sudden slip into the neglected terms of an opposition. An example could be that of the person whose rage suddenly turns to panic. Because of the intense focus on the state of rage, perhaps because of the cultural reinforcement of anger as preferable to fear, of assertion as preferable to withdrawal, the panic is felt as a hole into which one falls in a crisis. By using the cube as a model one is, first of all, invited to see fear as something more than a negative state of withdrawal as opposed to the more positive confrontational anger. Second, if one can see the new condition of fearful withdrawal as another aspect of the same relational network one can avoid disorientation. For example, whereas anger kept me in a confrontational relationship with someone, fear can maintain the same relationship but in terms of complementarity rather than competition. Wholeness and health would seem to depend on being able to relate to any other person as well as to oneself in both of these ways. "Catastrophe" would relate to an inability to navigate the change.

In his article in the *Scientific American* (April, 1976) E.C Zeeman elaborates a theory of catastrophe which explains sudden swings in behavior as catastrophes, failures to stand the tension of opposition. Fear suddenly turns to rage, for example, in dogs whose actions jump from flight to attack or vice versa. Analogies have been found in the behavior of crowds. A diagram of the phenomenon could resemble the following:

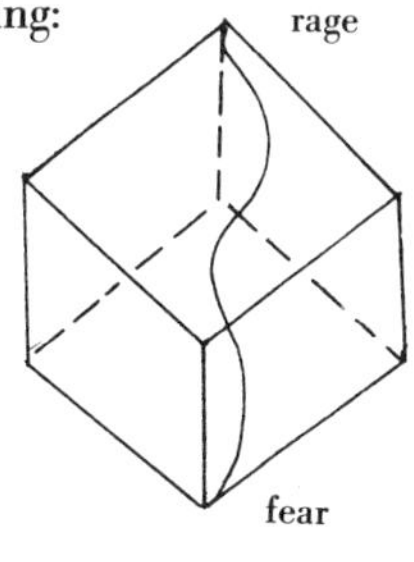

a 'wrinkle in the smooth surface of equilibrium which functions as a hole between opposites into which one can fall.

In his experiments with anorexia nervosa, in which the polar opposites are purging and gorging, the cure was to create a transitional "pocket" by means of a trance. Such a condition relieves the tension of symmetrical conflicts with oneself by returning the attention to oneself rather than the external conditions which trigger the opposing forces of fear/rage, gorging/purging, holding-in/letting-go. However, if one can see such tension as recalling one to awareness of one's inner center, one will have immediately a transitional "pocket" (see Cubal Analysis and Meditation). Such an inner state seems to be the key which can transform potentially destructive energies into creative ones.

Such an awareness presumes centeredness in one's sense of self as it exists within the cube, freed from identity with any simple pole. Thus the cube can serve as a balancing aid to anyone whose crisis involves an overidentification with any one of the axes: age, sex or morality. In this perspective the emphasis on sexuality of women, whose crises need to be symmetrical because concerned with sexual equality, becomes more important. Fear of one's sex (like fear of one's age or of others' judgement) can function as a barrier to the awareness essential to centeredness. Age, sex and morality then become a threshold to be passed in order to find new equilibrium amid the crises of change through natural or cultural processes. The promise is that of a new sense of identity rooted in one's self rather than in some thing external to one and in the release of new creative energy.

11
Cubal Analysis and Personal Analysis

In the psychological context of a group or private therapy the goal is to locate the area where the apparent problem lies, to help the person make the necessary distinctions and to integrate whatever material is being rejected. The inability to differentiate between opposites usually indicates a rejection of one of the terms of the pair. Here a variety of aids can be used such as pictures and or objects which seem to represent the character and or his or her qualities.

By using the various shaped dice one frees the imagination through play and permits the unconscious to emerge. By having the three forms: octahedron, hexahedron and tetrahedron, one has three tools by which to overcome blocks.

In cross-cultural or multi-cultural contexts one can use the dice to understand better the stereotypes through which one interprets the new culture. Often simply throwing the dice and comparing interpretation with a person from the other culture suffices to calm the anxiety provoked by differences. Although the theoretical framework is needed for interpretation, it cannot replace simple human recognition which is fostered by having the cube as a model for a network of relationships. The symmetry of the cube functions once again to counteract the skew of any given point of view or interpretation.

(Since each surface of the octahedron has a corresponding trigram in the *I Ching*, reference to the qualities of the given trigram can be used also when a dialogue between two people [and/or character types] is involved. Reference can be made to the hexagrams indicated by putting the two trigrams together in either or both of the two ways possible: x above or below y.)

A game played frequently with myself and/or my husband and/or another with whom I am involved personally started in the fall of 1979.

My first exploration then of the cube world was within my self. I would throw the die and meditate on the character type which landed face up. Usually there would be a series of images of real and/or fictional people who had or were functioning in my life in such a role. The function of the cube was to array the other character types around the one being directly confronted. In this way even when facing problem areas of myself or others I could situate myself in a network of relationships which kept the real or imagined threat in perspective.

A further elaboration of this procedure is to explore consciously all of the planes/apexes and the psychic characteristics they represent, while welcoming into oneself at any given time these diverse qualities and/or people as they flow through one's mind. Moving mentally between apparent opposites invites one to see their interrelationship; locating oneself and one's acquaintances in relation to these characteristics invites one to think in terms of continua rather than oppositions and to locate oneself on the coordinates somewhere inside the cube.

An obvious next move is playing cubally with those people whom one is close to and who continually emerge in one's imaginings. My husband and I have found using the cube together helpful in unraveling the knots which entangle from time to time any relationship.

In this situation we would each throw the die; the first person to throw would talk about how s/he perceived this character type and how s/he related to it—how s/he saw her/himself in that role. Then the partner would comment on his or her perceptions of the other in the role thrown. Then the second person would throw the die and proceed as the first had done. The perspective offered by the cube permitted us to see how our individual characteristics could interlock in such a way as to make us feel stuck. His role of the good old man could lock into my role of bad young girl, for example and make each of us feel frustrated and confined, even by that most socially reinforced of all roles: the good old man.

A further extension of this form of playing with the cube involves the partner as facilitator for the person exploring his or her psyche. Here questions probing areas one might not otherwise approach and encouragement in facing difficult areas are essential. Total blockage with one character type can be overcome often by looking at its total polar opposite. In spite of the obvious mathematical symmetry of the die and the model, it often takes another person to point out when in fact one has reduced a three-dimensional type, let's say the good young man, to a one-dimensional person by only talking about the characteristics one associates with goodness and ignoring sexuality and youth.

The perfect mathematical completeness of the model invites one to perceive one's biases. It also invites one to see the biases around one. In the context of gaming, making a decision, taking a position means accepting a bias. Accepting a relationship means also encountering another's bias.

12
Cubal Analysis and Interpersonal Play

Goal: Use cube
Get feedback in variety of ways.

Materials: Seven cubal dice of same dimensions—octahedrons

1. *Goal:* To maximize feedback, divide group into six subgroups (one extra cube)

Strategy: Each subgroup plays by a different set of rules
For example—1) explore self
- a) with a helper
- b) without a helper

2) explore relationship
- a) both assume the roles
- b) take turns being facilitator for the other

3) explore situation
- a) with a partner
- b) without a partner

Assumptions:
1) the rolled face is part of oneself; one then talks to oneself
2) the rolled face is a person in one's life with whom one then converses
3) the rolled face is part of oneself or another or an impersonal force viewed from the perspective of a given life situation

Partner possibilities—assume role throw of die
act as facilitator

Each subgroup selects a member who will oversee group's activities

b) lead discussion afterward briefly

c) present a common denominator to the whole group

Discussion

2. *Goal:* To maximize projector

Strategy: Pair up with someone

whom you know at least a bit

who will act as facilitator

who will comment on junctions/disjunctions s/he sees between his/her perceptions and your perceptions-

3. *Goal:* To maximize variety and ease

Strategy: Present as a quiet invitation to explore oneself alone or with others according to own rules

13
Cubal Analysis and Teachers

At a three-day workshop for in service teachers I played a game I enjoyed, which involved Kate Chopin's *Story of an Hour* and yielded interesting results. The first part of the story ends with a woman exploring a sense of freedom at her husband's death and wishing that life might be long. Then there is a knock on her door. I asked the participants to throw the die and fantasize the conclusion. Once this was done I asked them to comment on Chopin's version which ended with the woman dying of a heart attack when her husband returns and to compare their ending with hers.

There were about sixty participants in all who came from the local public high school system. Those who came to my workshop formed three different groups. The first group was composed of people I knew. All of the men in this group threw the bad young man and fantasized the end of the woman's freedom through the agency of their character, either by death or seduction. The women thought she would be cared for by her father—the good old man. In comparison to the other groups this was the most charitable toward feminine freedom.

In the second group, there were a few initial attempts at covert aggression which, however, seemed normal among teachers who are in the habit of being listened to rather than of listening. Here the increased aggression showed itself in a majority of people who fantasized the death of the woman and one young man who explicitly said that he felt uneasy when faced with the image of a free woman. Although this group did exactly what the first did, it took a bit longer and there were fewer comments and/or questions.

The third group was obviously less comfortable between the presentation of the theory and the games. With the literature game there was an even greater majority fantasizing the demise of the heroine, stating explicitly that such freedom is intolerable. Again one or two women saw her being "saved" by the good father or father-in-law. The overall response was one of considerable interest, which was implicit in the fact that all of these teachers were willing to be taught cubal gaming for a total of five and a half hours.

If one were to analyze in cubal terms the shape of Chopin's story, one would have to see that those who sided with her death were reinforcing certain standard cultural values; however, interestingly, none who posited the intervention of the good father fantasized her death, whereas, in the story it is just this confrontation between the good old man and the bad young woman that is too much for the woman. Having passed through the "room of her own", she feels young because of the future she sees in front of her. She also feels free partly perhaps in response to sudden feelings of release by the good husband, the good old man, who could nonetheless judge and so whose absence can liberate her sense of morality. Feelings of youth are then related to freedom from judgements. When she sees her husband, guilt for her freedom which was a function of his death rushes in. Thus in cubal terms we have a crisis situation: the good old man, the providing husband, returns and confronts, in her eyes, not the good old woman he had married but the bad young girl. There are two polar relationships and between them create a central axis around the cube, the room, one's standard orientation, spins like a top. Between polar characters there is nothing to relate the two. She was suddenly a stranger to her husband and to her former self—and her weak heart could not take it.

14
Cubal Analysis and Language Learning

Simple Present

In the following language games the cubal die functions to distance the students from their sense of self such that verbal participation in the classroom is facilitated.

Choose a partner.
Throw the die and assume the character you have thrown.
You (as your character) are consulting a psychiatrist— —your partner.
Your psychiatrist must ask you all about your life, habits, preferences, hobbies, vacations...to get to know you.
Examples: Where do you live? What is your favorite food?....
Switch roles.

Present Continuous

Choose a partner and throw the die, same as above.
Your partner, in his/her character, drops by while you are busy and wants to get you talking.
Example: What are you doing? What are you thinking about? Why are you laughing? What are you cooking?....
Switch roles.

First conditional
(present/future)

Choose a partner.
Throw the die and assume the character you have thrown.
Your partner does the same.
Your partner is asking you about your future prospects.
Example: What will you do if/when you get out of school?
How will you live if you can't find a job?....
Switch roles.

Second Conditional
(past/conditional)

Same as above.
You are giving advice to your partner: if I were you,...
Your partner may have questions: why would you...
Or, you are telling your partner what you would do if you met him/her by chance on the street.
Switch roles.

Third Conditional
(past perfect/conditional perfect)

Same as above.
You are at the police station reporting the accident of a friend.
You are blaming yourself for the accident, in answer to the policeman's/woman's questions.
Example: If I had been more careful...Why would it have been different...
Switch roles.

Present Perfect

Choose a partner.
Throw the die.
Assume the role of the character thrown.
Your partner also throws the die and assumes the role of the character s/he has thrown.
You (as your character) are applying for a job offered by your partner (as the character s/he has thrown).
Describe what you have done up to the present which suits you for this job. Your partner can ask questions.
Switch roles.
(Of course, you must first decide what kind of employment possibilities exist between your two character types.)

Past Perfect

Choose a partner.
Throw the die. Your partner does the same.
In the roles of the characters each one has thrown, you and your partner have just met and begun an important relationship (for better or for worse).
Describe in a dialogue what life was like before you met: how much better/worse life was before your partner came into it, what you used to do but has now changed...
Example: Before I met you, I had never been so miserable/happy...
By the time I met you, I had already done many things...

Simple future

Choose a partner.
Throw the die and assume the character you have thrown.
Your partner does the same.
You, in your character, are consulting a fortune teller—your partner. S/he tells you all about your future, in answer to your questions.
Example: How many children will I have? Where will I live?....
Switch roles.

Simple past

Choose a partner, same as above.
You, in your character, are telling a fairy-tale to your partner, who, like a child, asks many questions.
Example: Once upon a time, Little Red Riding Hood went out...
—Why did she go out?...
Or: you and your partner were supposed to have met yesterday,but you couldn't find him/her. You want to find out what happened.
Example: Why weren't you there? —I was...
Switch roles.

Character Exploration

Throw the die.
How does your character dress? How does s/he look?
How does your character express: pleasure?
pain?
sorrow—at what?
anger—at what?
joy—at what?
fear—of what?
pity—for what?
scorn—of what?
What does your character eat? What recipes does s/he know?
What does s/he do on vacation? In his/her free time as a hobby?
Describe what your character does exactly.
How would character: ask for directions/advice?
give directions/advice?
entertain guests?
be rude/polite?
Describe your character's friends/ideal partner
family
job(s)
colleagues
What is your character's favorite entertainment?
sport?
book?
movie?
vacation spot?

restaurant?
costume at Halloween?
historical period?

What is his/her most important or greatest ambition in life?
What kind of pet(s) does your character have/like?
What does s/he always
sometimes
never
usually eat?
often do?
rarely listen to?

What weather does s/he like best?
Comparisons:
Divide the class into groups of two or three.
Each person throws the die, describes his or her character type in terms of certain variables (family, dwelling size, etc.)
Each group then compares the characters described in terms of the variables.

Having finished any unit on a given situation, the students have learned the vocabulary and structures which are part of the lesson, for example, "At the Railway Station". As a form of review the teacher can

1. put a transparency of a railway station on the wall, ask each student to throw the die and describe the station from the point of view of that character type.
2. having the students keep the character types already thrown, the teacher can then divide the class into small groups and have them act out simple sketches of what might happen among such a mix of characters at a railway station.

The first part can be done orally or in writing and prepares for the second part.

15
Cubal Analysis and Literature

Since age, sex and "morality" or the need to make judgements are inescapable human realitites, it is certain that they will be found in fiction. In addition, being such essential parameters of human life, they can furnish useful mediations between individuals and fiction.

Their appeal to adolescents ought even to be greater than to adults. We are all in the process of navigating our ways into a world not of our making, therefore potentially full of alien, arbitrary judgements not only concerned with separating the good from the bad, but with defining appropriate behavior for individuals of different sexes and ages.

By using then such fundamental categories, one can begin to tame some of the more ubiquitous areas of prejudice. Because the terms are so simple, one must participate in the elaboration of their meaning, only to discover what "I" think being young means is not the same as what my friends think. In addition one can be sure not only of finding these factors in all character portrayals but also of finding their particular embodiment revealing both in terms of the author and of his or her epoch.

Looking at social stereotypes can help one create his or her own categories and see them in relation to "standard" ones. It does no harm to learn for example that among a number of adolescents good old women are described as caring for animals and/or are sick whereas good old men care for humans, for example, by teaching, but physically are not different from good young men, i.e. their reactional habits are unchanged.

Taking sex, age and "morality" as parameters for analysis shares characteristics with the other fictions one is trying to understand.

In trying to link any theory to any reality, two principal factors are involved. One is simplification: just as a map simplifies the terrain it represents, so a theory reduces irregularities to common links. The second is viability: just as a road permits many to travel over it, so a theory opens new areas to others. A theory provides some common lines which help one individual relate to another in spite of differences, and which even help one to relate to oneself, in spite of the different idea one may have of one's self.

A theory then is, like a map or a fiction, a form of mediating between individuals and individual experiences. In terms of literature the characters are not people and so they permit us to experiment and experience imaginatively, without consequences in daily life. The criterion implicit is how "viable" the fiction is: is this a system of signs that can help one navigate in Thonex only, in Geneva, Switzerland, in Europe, in the West, etc.? Does a fiction give me insight simultaneously into myself, into other humans—including perhaps the author and into its structure? Can the parameters of Cubal Analysis provide a metafiction which facilitates insight into myself and others by means of a given piece of fiction?

Every act of fiction then implies in its parameters those conditions in opposition to which its ordered world (of poetry or prose or whatever) assumes its form. Experience is the parameter of the map and vice versa. Disorder is necessary for order to emerge. One can approach the problem why an author chose as s/he did a certain evaluation, by exploring the alternatives.

Throw the die: at a crucial moment what would a character such as the one you threw have done, had s/he been able to intervene.

A gift of reading fiction is to slow life down so one can look at it with a clearer perspective than is normally possible when one is in the midst of one's life.

Since parameters of age, sex and morality are inescapable realities, how they are represented can give one access to a framework for the fictional world.

Throw the die: where is the character type which you threw present? Individually? As a social force?

To continue the map/road analogy, here are two kinds of less successful tourists: Type A buys a Eurail Pass and regularly sleeps each night on the train and, gets off where ever s/he wakes up: since s/he has read nothing about the country visited, s/he spends the day wandering around and talking to fellow tourists. "Seeing" England becomes, for example, a series of Lower Exeter Falls and doesn't even include London. Type B buys many guidebooks and rushes intently to all the starred attractions. Once there s/he sits and reads about whatever famous place and then leaves. S/he is like the couple that visited a famous zoo in winter. They went carefully from cage to cage reading the signs, perhaps not noticing that the animals were inside their house and not visible.

The following text can serve as an example of how Cubal Analysis can serve as a framework in analyzing a given piece of fiction. In choosing *Dreamsnake* by Vonda McIntyre I cannot avoid the personal element: I like the book and the author, who also shares my interest in *Star Trek*. In addition I hope there are elements of public revelance in a discussion of it. By applying cubal terms to it I wish to focus on ways in which it offers a fresh perspective on issues of concern to women today, especially to women on the move.

The choice of science fiction is itself significant in terms of the needs of women writers. The main plot of the book concerns the "proving year" or initiation of the protagonist, Snake, a healer. During this time she must earn the name she both was given and chose at the end of her studies by leaving her native country and discovering what it means to encounter alien systems of discrimination and judgement. Already we have in a new setting a problem central to women today: how does one live in an alien world? How can one affirm oneself as a woman in a world dominated by man-made categories—particularly when these categories define women in terms of men. The feeling often expressed by women is that of an ineffective bystander left in the backwater of dishes and diapers while real events are taking place in the arena of life. Such a feeling can find correspondence in the individual facing a foreign culture of the non-initiate confronted by rules of an unknown game. However nice this crossing into the unknown has been made, one can assume an active role of creator oneself in a pluralistic world freed from an ethnocentric concept of good versus bad, mythologizer versus mythologized.

Significantly Snake falls in love during her brief stay in the first foreign culture she is called to as healer. Their relationship is that of partners in the healing Snake was called there to perform. Nonetheless this episode opens the area specifically dealing with sex and femininity. In this instance we see the affective dimension of sexual attraction, which because taken separately lets us later see other dimensions of sexuality more clearly. The next one comes when she finds herself loved by a man who has no confidence in his own biocontrol. (In this society all birth control is done by conscious biocontrol). Snake in having a sexual relationship with him becomes his teacher and healer by helping him acquire the biocontrol necessary to his identity and positive self-image. The third encounter with an element of her sexuality comes when she meets Melissa, a scarred brutalized girl whose values and talents go only to enhance the man who exploits her. Here they mutually chose each other as mother and daughter and in doing so affirm the relationship both as union and as separation: they are bound together but as conscious participants. This seems to me to be a significant advance over

Demeter and Persephone or Amor and Psyche as myths for feminine consciousness. In both these myths the daughter succumbs to unconscious union with the mother. In so far as the mother and daughter do not differentiate themselves from each other the daughter as feminine consciousness does not fully emerge. As Anne Sexton said, "A woman is her mother, that's the main thing"—to be transcended. I also find this an advance over the male myth of emerging consciousness, i.e. the Oedipus situation canonized by Freud. Here the son, the consciousness, must kill the father of the unconscious (as tradition) to emerge in the end; the danger, however, is that consciousness in cutting itself off from the unconscious destroys the source of its future growth. By taking sexuality apart into its affective element, McIntyre has gone a long way to creating a figure of an effective woman. By seeing sexuality as an assembly of component parts we can find ourselves once again in a pluralistic rather than a bipolar world.

Of the three categories age, sex and discrimination the first, age is the most primary and personal. Separated from the social roles and expectations which usually surround its age has essentially to do with the physical limits of our bodies. And this is the way in which it is treated in *Dreamsnake*: Snake's training as healer has required her to develop immunities to the venom of the poisonous snakes which are the agents of her healing and her companions. Although dragons have been the ultimate expression of autonomous and dangerous unconscious powers, snakes share such characteristics on a more domesticated level. Traditionally, and characteristically of our tendency to bipolar thinking, dragons either slay or are slain. Snake, however, just as she has a partnership relationship with her lover and her daughter, has it also with her snakes. The crucial turning point of the novel takes place in the heart of evil, in a snake pit, exploited by a megalomaniac. Here although the collective venom of these creatures risks killing her she realizes that she cannot kill them and be herself. Her bodily limits, already modified by her training, become the vehicle for her healing vision and her awareness of its essential value. The snakes in question, which she needs professionally, have never reproduced in captivity, and the snakepit in which she finds herself is the first time such a place of their natural reproduction has been found. At the outermost limits of her physical and psy hological being she has a vision of the snakes reproducing in the cold and in threes, contrary to the anthropecentric notion of the cozy twosome. She will take back with her the key to raising the snakes whose former rarity, not human cruelty, made healers an elite. Her survival also depends on a plurality of factors: her love for her daughter, her training as a healer which has made snakes companions, and her personal will to survive and assert herself, in which she must now also recognize those characteristics she hates in the man who put her in the pit—i.e. the desire to humiliate and destroy in order to gain power. This, too, is part of awareness attendent on her healing vision.

Without going into the many details of the social structure of the alternative universe which of course minimizes prescriptive or punitive judgements and valorizes individuals of both sexes and all ages, we can find, I hope, in this very brief view of one figure some answers to important questions asked by women today. In taking the terms of cubal analysis as a three-dimensional lens we are automatically encouraged to move beyond the limits of a bipolar world with its definitions of good versus bad because bad is absence of good, of masculine versus feminine because the latter is once again only the absence of the former and of youth versus age because once again the latter is just a running down, a diminution of the former. By distributing these qualities on the axes of a cube, each is given its appropriate space and function in a universe as pluralistic as there are points of coordination among the three axes. Thus the tendency to fall into the trap of bipolar opposition is avoided in two ways: first of all we are invited to arrange our world in terms of the three cubal coordinates; then in terms of these coordinates we are encouraged to think in terms of continua rather than contradictions. Thus this process assures that we not only perceive in terms of gradations but also in terms of fully conceived coordinates: bad is not just the absence of good, nor feminine the lack of the masculine, nor age just a waning of youth. Age, feminine sexuality, and evil all become bearers of meaning.

In August 1980 in order to contribute to a gaming convention in Geneva, I had to select which were the most relevant strategies and goals. This was the first time that I used the cube in gaming with a group of strangers rather than with persons I would see regularly. Since each game has to be constructed as a function of a given context, I first of all had to guess at the factors which would provide the constants for this group.

My assumptions were therefore that we were all strangers, that we as gamers had a certain facility with fantasy, that we were adults and that we shared some common language—French or English. Therefore I presumed a certain individual independence of action within a context but relied on the die itself to provide the necessary common denominator of a structure within which we could function without distracting from our differences.

I asked each participant to throw a die and to write the character type s/he received on the top of a piece of paper. Each person then wrote a sketch of such a person, who could be real or fictitious. On the basis of these personal sketches I asked all those exploring a common character type to form a group and to compare the ways in which they envisioned their personages. After half an hour in the subgroups we returned to one large group to identify the common elements in the composite portraits evolved in each subgroup and those which were functions of various individuals.

We began to compare differences one axis at a time and had time only to compare sexual opposites, the good old woman with the good old man, which resulted in the generalization that the goodness of the woman was expressed in her caring for animals in a fairly private world, whereas that of the man was to express his wisdom in a public domain. When morality was taken as the target variable, it becomes a matter of mastery versus domination: the good old person had expertise and/or wisdom to offer whereas the bad old person sought to dominate others. Once again here the woman exercised her power within a private world and the man in a public one.

General feedback indicated that in general the participants felt particular resonance with the character types they threw. While some said during the session that they would probably have felt this intimacy with any of the types, others told me afterward that theirs had had special personal relevance to their lives at that time. For example, middle-aged men in mid-life crisis felt that throwing the bad young girl was particularly relevant. Of the fifteen throws one third resulted in the bad young girl: (Could an imperfect die be implicated or are male mid-life crises on the up-surge??)

Another general factor was that they all but one out of fifteen felt that as a result of playing this game they had come to know each other quickly and well. From here on they had clear notions of those with whom they would wish to pursue relationships and those whom they would prefer to avoid.

16
A Consciousness-raising Cubal Questionaire

Name:
Address:
Occupation:
Age:
Sex and/or gender:
Social Identity:
Situation in which you used a cube:

What were the issues initially involved in the given situation:
What happened when you had to think in terms of three issues:
What happened when you had to think in terms of continua:
Identify the poles of the axes used:
What was the alternative thrown:
What was your reaction to the alternative thrown:
What was the outcome of the situation:
If you were doing this in the context of a group:

identify the participants
identify their throws
identify their reactions to their own throws:
to the throws of others:

Concluding unscientific comments:
I will welcome your feedback.

Bibliography

Albarn, Keith, et al. *Diagram.* London: Thames and Hudson, 1977.

Albee, Edward. "Box." *Tiny Alice, Box and Quotations from Chairman Mao-Tse-Tung.* Harmondsworth: Penguin Books, 1971.

Aquinas, Thomas. "Summa Theologica," *Introduction to Contemporary Civilization in The West,* vol. I. New York: Columbia University Press, 1960.

Arguelles, Jose. *Mandala.* Boulder: Shambala Press, 1975.

Assagioli, Robert. *The Act of Will.* London: Wildwood House, 1973.

Atwood, Margaret. *Surfacing.* New York: Popular Library, 1976.

Becker, Ernest. *The Denial of Death.* New York: The Free Press, 1973.

Blair, John G. *The Confidence Man in Modern Fiction.* London: Vision Press, 1979.

Boiron, N.M. *Les regimes et les sanctions de la prostitution dans l'histoire devant le droit, devant l'opinion.* Nancy: Bergor-Levrault, 1926.

Castenada, Carlos. *A Separate Reality.* New York: Simon and Schuster, 1971.

Castenada, Carlos. *Tales of Power.* New York: Pocket Books, 1976.

Castenada, Carlos. *The Teachings of Don Juan: A Yaqui Way of Knowledge.* New York: Ballantine Books, 1969.

Budapest Z. *The Feminist Book of Lights and Shadows.* Venice, Calif.: Luna Publications, 1976.

Capra, Fritjof. *The Tao of Physics.* Boulder: Shambala, 1975.

Chesler, Phyllis. *Women and Madness.* New York: Avon Books, 1973.

Chang, Chung-yuan. *Tao; A New Way of Thinking.* New York: Perennial Library, 1977.

Claremont de Castillejo, Irene. *Knowing Woman.* New York: Harper Colophon Books, 1974.

Daly, Mary. *Beyond God The Father.* Boston: Beacon Press, 1974.

Delaney, Janice, et al. *The Curse: A Cultural History of Menstruation.* New York: Mentor Books, 1977.

Celeuze, Gilles, et al. *Dialogues.* Paris: Flammarion, 1977.

Des Pres, Terrence. *The Survivor.* New York: Pocket Books, 1977.

Downing, Chris. "Separating and Connecting: The Rhythm and Its Manifestation." *Inner Light,* (Fall 1978).

Dreifus, Claudia. *Seizing Our Bodies.* New York: Vintage Books, 1978.

Dubois, Abbe J.A. *Hindu Manners, Customs and Ceremonies.* Oxford: Clarendon Press, 1906.

Dworken, Andrea. "Marx and Gandhi Were Liberals — Feminism and The Radical Left." *American Report,* 1973.

Edinger, Edward. "The New Myth of Meaning." *Quadrant* 1977.
Edwards, Allen. *The Jewel in The Lotus.* New York: Lancer Books, 1969.
Ehrenreich, Barbara, et al. "Witches, Midwives and Nurses." *Glass Mountain Pamphlet,* No.1.
Eliade, Mircea. *Myths, Dreams & Mysteries.* Glasgow: Fontana, 12968.
Eliade, Mircea. *Rites and Symbols of Initiation.* New York: Harper &Row, 1958.
Ellmann, Mary. *Thinking About Women.* New York: Harcourt Brace Janovich, 1968.
Encyclopedia Britannica: Micropedia vol. IV. London: Helen Hemingway Benton, Publisher, 1973-74.
Engler, Barbara. "Freud's Sexual Politics: Heresy or Heroism?" *Anima,* 2, No. 2 (Spring Equinox 1976).
Fallot, T. *La femme esclave.* Paris: Libraire Fischbacher, 1884.
Fischer, Roland, and Rhead, John. "The Logical and the Intuitive." *Main Currents,* Nov.-Dec., 1974, vol. 31, No. 2.
Flaceliere, Robert. *L'amour en Grece.* Paris: Hachette, 1960.
Franklin, Bruce H. *Future Perfect,* rev. ed. New York: Oxford University Press, 1978.
Freud, Sigmund. *Civilizations and its Discontents.* New York: Norton, 1961.
Freud, Sigmund. *New Introductory Lectures on Psychocoanalysis.* New York: Norton, 1965.
Freud, Sigmund. *The Origins of Psychoanalysis.* New York: Doubleday, 1975.
Freud, Sigmund. "Psychanalyse," *Le Revue de Geneve,* No. 7., Geneve: Societe Anonyme des Editeurs, 1921.
Freud, Sigmund. *Totem and Taboo.* Middlesex: Penguin Books, 1938.
Freud, Sigmund. *Trois essais sur la sexualite.* Paris: Gallimard, 1932.
Friday, Nancy. *My Mother, Myself.* New York: Dell Books, 1978.
Gardner, Martin. *The Ambidexterous Universe.* New York: Basic Books, 1964.
Givry, Grillot de. *Witchcraft, Magic and Alchemy.* New York: Houghton Mifflin, 1931.
Goleman, Daniel. "Holographic Memory." *Psychology Today,* 12., No. 9 (Feb. 1979)
Gross, Rita. "On Being A Religious Jewish Woman." *Anima,* vol. 1. No. 1 (Fall Equinox).
Guggenbuhl, Craig. *Power in The Helping Professions,* ed. James Hillman. New York: Spring Publications, 1971.
Hall, Calvin. *A Primer of Freudian Psychology.* New York: Mentor Books, 1955.
Hall, Edward T. *Beyond Culture.* New York: Anchor Books, 1977.
Hall, Edward T. *The Hidden Dimension.* New York: Anchor Books, 1969.
Hall, Edward T. *The Silent Language.* New York: Anchor Books, 1973.
Hannah, Barbara. *Jung: His Life Work.* New York: McGraw-Hill, 1977.
Harding, Esther. *Woman's Mysteries.* New York: Bantam Books, 1973.
Harris, Thomas. *I'm OK, You're OK.* London: Pan Books, 1973.
Havens, Joseph, et al. "Solitude; In-one-self-ness; Transcendance." *Inner Light,*vol. 37, No. 85 (Fall 1974).
Henriques, Fernando Louis. *Prostitution and Society: A Survey,* vol. I London: MacGibban and Kee, 1962.
Hillman, James. *Loose Ends.* Zurich: Spring, 1975.
Hillman, James, and Roscher, W.H. *Pan and The Nightmare.* Zurich: Spring, Dunquin Series 4, 1972.
Hillman, James. "The Great Mother, Her Son, Her Hero and The Puer." *Fathers and Mothers.* Zurich: Spring, 1973.
The I Ching, trans. Richard Wilhelm and Gary F. Baynes, 3rd ed. Princeton: Princeton University Press, Bollingen Series XIX, 1967.
Irigaray, Luce. *Speculum de l'autre femme.* Paris: Ed. de Minuit, 1974.

Iskin, Ruth. "Feminist Education at The Feminist Studio Workshop." Mimeographed. n.d.
Jacobi, Jolande. *Complex, Archetype, Symbol.* Princeton: Princeton University Press, Bollingen Series LVII, 1971.
Jacquith, Cindy, et al. *Which Way for the Women's Movement?* New York: Pathfinder Press, 1977.
James, Muriel and Jongeward, Dorothy. *Born to Win.* Reading, Mass.: Addison-Wesley, 1971.
Jayakar, R.B.K. "Prostitution and Immoral Traffic in India." *Social Welfare in India.* New Dehli: Government of India, n.d.
Gensen, Sorens. *Dualism and Demonolgy,* Munksgaard, 1966.
Jinks, William. *The Celluloid Literature.* 2nd ed. Beverly Hills, Calif.: Glencoe Press, 1974.
Johnson, Robert. *She: Understanding Feminine Psychology.* New York: Perennial Library, 1977.
Johnson, Robert. *He.* King of Prussia, Pa.: Religious Publishing Co., 1974.
Jolley, J.L. *The Fabric of Knowledge,* London: Duckworth, 1973.
Jones, Ernest. *The Life and Work of Sigmund Freud.* New York: Basic Books, 1961.
Jung, C.G. *The Collected Works of C.G. Jung,* ed. Sir Herbert Read, et al., trans. R.F.C. Hull. New York: Pantheon Books, Bollingen Series XX, 1953-76.
Jung, C.G. *Memories, Dreams, Reflections.,* ed. Aniela Jaffee, trans. Richard Winston. Glasgow: Fountain Books, 1977.
Jung, Emma. *Animus and Anima.* Zurich: Spring Publications, 1957.
Kino, F.F. "Aliens' Paranoid Reactions." *Uprooting and After...,* ed. Charles Zwingman and Maria Pfister Ammende. New York: Springer, 1973.
Kramer, Samuel Noah. *The Sacred Marriage Rite.* Bloomington: Indiana University Press, 1969.
Kuhn, Thomas. *The Structure of Scientific Revolution.* Chicago: University of Chicago Press, 1962.
LaForge, Paul. *Research Profiles with Community Language Learning.* Apple River, Illinois: Counselling-learning Institutes, 1975.
Lakoff, Robin. *Language and Women's Place.* New York: Harper Colophon Books, 1975.
Lamphere, Louise. *Woman, Culture and Society.* Stanford: Stanford University Press, 1974.
Lao Tzu. *Tao Teh Ching: The Way and Its Power,* trans. Arthur Waley. London: Allen & Unwin, 1934.
Leach, Edmund. *Claude Levi-Strauss.* Harmondsworth: Penguin Books, 1976.
Leach, Edmund. *Culture and Communication.* Cambridge: Cambridge University, 1976.
Lessing, Doris. *A Small Personal Voice.* New York: Vintage, 1975.
Lessing, Doris. *The Golden Notebook.* New York: Bantam Books, 1973.
Lessing, Doris. *The Memoirs of A Survivor.* London: Picador, 1976.
Lewinsohn, Richard. *A History of Sexual Customs.* London: Longmans Green, 1958.
Lobell, Mimi. "Spatial Archetypes." *Quadrant,* 10, No. 2 (Winter 1977)
Lockhart, Russell A. "Cancer in Myth and Dream." *Spring* 1977.
Lowen, Alexander. *Bioenergetics.* New York: Penguin Books, 1976.
Macy, Joanna. "Perfection of Wisdom: Mother of All Buddhas." *Anima,* vol. 3, No. 1 (1977).
Mathur, A.S. et al. *Prostitutes and Prostitution.* Agra: Ram Prasad and Sons, 1965.

Matlack, Jean Y. "A Life of Study of A Psychotherapist: Marjorie Murray Burtt." Diss. University of Massachusetts 1976.
Mead, Margaret. *Male and Female*. New York: Laurel Editions, 1968.
Meagher, Robert E. "Strangers at The Gate." *Parabola*, 2, No. 4.
Miller, Jean Baker. *Toward A New Psychology of Women*. Harmondsworth: Penguin Books, 1978.
Millet, Kate. *The Prostitution Papers: A Candid Dialogue*. N.Y.: Avon 1973.
Neumann, Erich. *Depth Psychology and A New Ethic*. New York: Harper Torchbooks, 1973.
Neumann, Erich. *The Origins and History of Consciousness*. Princeton: Princeton University Press, Bollingen Series XLII, 1954.
Nowacki, Werner. "The Idea of A Structure of Reality." *Main Currents*, vol. 31, No. 2 (Nov.-Dec.).
Osmond, Humphry. "The Mechanical Model in Psychiatry." *Hospital and Community Psychiatry*: A Journal of the American Psychiatric Association., vol. 21, No. 9 (September 1970).
Payer, Mary. "Is Traditional Scholarship Value Free? Toward A Critical Theory." *The Scholar and The Feminist IV: Connecting Theory, Practice and Values*. Barnard College, New York: papers from the morning Conference sponsored by the Woman's Center, 1972.
Perls, Frederick S. *Gestalt Therapy Verbatim*. New York: Bantam Books, 1972.
Perls, Frederick S. *In and Out The Garbage Pail*. New York: Bantam Books, 1971.
Piercy, Marge. *Woman On The Edge of Time*. New York: Fawcett Crest, 1976.
Plath, Sylvia.ound. At the outermost limits of her physical and psychological being she has a vision of the snakes reproducing in the cold *The Bell Jar*. New York: Bantam Books, 1972.
Plaza, Monique. "Phallomorphic Power and The Psychology of 'Woman'." *Ideology and Consciousness*, No. 4 (Autumn 1978).
Progoff, Ira. *At A Journel Workshop*. New York: Dialogue House Library, 1975.
Progoff, Ira. *Jung's Psychology and Its Social Meaning*. New York: Anchor Books, 1973.
Quest: A Feminist Quarterly, special issue: International Feminism, Vol. IV, No. 2. (Winter 1978).
Rogeat, Marcel. *Moeurs et Prostitution*. Paris: Nouvelles Editions Latines, 1935.
Rogers, Carl. *Freedom to Learn*. Columbus, Ohio: Charles E. Merrill Publishing Co., 1969.
Savramis, Demosthenes. *The Satirizing of Woman*. Garden City, New York: Doubleday and Co., 1974.
Scott, George. *A History of Prostitution*. London: Werner Laurie, Cabban House, 1936.
Shepard, Martin. *Fritz: An Intimate Portrait of Fritz Perls and Gestalt Therapy*. New York: Saturday Review Press, 1975.
Shiner, Larry E. "Sacred Space, Profane Space, Human Space." *IAAR*, vol. XL (1972).
Sperber, Dan. *Rethinking Symbolism*. Cambridge: Cambridge University Press, 1975.
Srinagesh, Sampurna. "Some Thoughts on Women's Liberation for India." Unpublished manuscript, n.d.
Stein, Robert. *Incest and Human Love*. Baltimore: Penguin Books, 1974.
Steiner, Claude M. *Scripts People Live*. New York: Bantam Books, 1975.
Stevens, John O. *Gestalt Is*. New York: Bantam Books, 1977.

Strouse, Jean, ed. *Women and Analysis.* New York: Laurel Edition, 1975.
Therese, Marie. *Histoire d'une prosituee.* Paris: Collection Femme, Editions Gauthier, 1964.
Tyrwhitt, Jacqueline. "The Moving Eye." *Exploration in Communication.*Boston: Beacon Press, 1972.
Ulanov, Ann and Barry. *Religion and The Unconscious.* Philadelphia: The Westminster Press, 1975.
Valenti, Jack. "The Art and Business of Films." *International* Education and Cultural Exchange, vol. XIII, No. 3 (Winter 1978).
Von Franz, Marie. *The Feminine in Fairytales.* Zurich: Spring Publications, 1972.
Von Franz, Marie. *Interpretation of Fairytales.* Zurich: Spring Publications, 1973.
Watzlawick, Paul. *How Real Is Real?* New York: Vintage Books, 1977.
Weaver, Rix. *The Old Wise Woman.* New York: C.G. Jung Foundation, 1973.
Weininger, Otto. *Sex and Character.* London: William Heinemann, 1906.
Whan, Michael. "'Don Juan,' Trickster." *Spring* 1978.
Whitbeck, Caroline. "The Maternal Instinct." Paper presented at the Regional Meeting of the Society for Women in Philosophy, Amherest Mass., Oct. 1972.
Wilber, Ken. "The Spectrum of Consciousness." *Main Currents*, vol. 31, No. 2 (Nov. Dec. 1974).
Winick, Charles, et al. "Prostitutes." *Psychology Today* (Feb. 1972).
Winick, Charles. "Prostitutes 'Clients' Perception of the Prostitutes and of Themselves." *The Lively Commerce: Prostitution in the United States.* New York: Quadrangle, 1971.
Zeeman, E.C. "Catastrophe Theory," *Scientific American*, April 1976.